INSIGHTFUL TIPS FOR THE UNIQUE, "MATURE" SINGLE
(IN HER WAIT FOR "MR RIGHT")

By Andrea Best

xulon
PRESS

Copyright © 2007 by Andrea Best

Insightful Tips for the Unique "Mature" Single
by Andrea Best

Printed in the United States of America

ISBN-13: 978-1-60034-491-6
ISBN-10: 1-60034-491-7

All rights reserved solely by the author. The author guarantees all contents are original and do not infringe upon the legal rights of any other person or work. No part of this book may be reproduced in any form without the permission of the author. The views expressed in this book are not necessarily those of the publisher.

Unless otherwise indicated, Bible quotations are taken from the *King James* Version *(KJV), New Living Translation (NLT), The Amplified Bible (TAB), The Message (TM) and The New International* Version *(NIV)*.

www.xulonpress.com

To

Anna,

I hope you had a lovely birthday.

May God continue to bless Your Life!

You are a blessed woman of God - He will use you mightily.

All Best

Jeremiah 29v11.

23/4/07.

TABLE OF CONTENTS

Introduction vii

1. Let's Be Honest With Ourselves 13
2. You Are Unique! You Were Born to Be You ... 21
3. Alone But Not Lonely 29
4. Live Your Life 'in the Now' 35
5. Don't Stay Bitter – Get Better 41
6. God Longs to Be Your One and Only
   True Love 51
7. Pamper Yourself – Who Else Will? 63
8. But God, My Biological Clock Is
   Ticking … Loudly! 73
9. To Be or Not to Be – That Is the Question 83
10. Square Pegs Don't Fit Into Round Holes 89
11. 'No Ringy, No Thingy!' – Raise Your
    Expectations, Because You're Worth So
    Much More! 99
12. Did You Know That False Perception Can
    Lead to Deception? 109
13. For Every 'Ruth' There Is a 'Boaz' 119
14. Take a Leaf Out of the Book of "Mrs.
    Proverbs 31" 129
15. By the Way, What Are the Men Doing? 137
16. This Too Will Pass 145

INTRODUCTION

At last, here is a book written specifically for you, the mature single woman. If you find that you fit into the category of being a single woman who has reached the age of 30-plus and at present have not yet found your 'Mr. Right,' please read on; you will be encouraged.

There's absolutely nothing to be ashamed of or to feel inferior about in any way; I'm one of the women in that category, so this book was personally birthed from my heart. I believe that qualifies me to be empathetic to your cause. My objective in writing this book is to offer you hope and encouragement, rather than doom and gloom, during this challenging season in your life. I say challenging because it seems more common now than, say, in the 80s and 90s, that the Church has a number of mature single women. However, if we are honest with ourselves and if given the choice, the majority of us would not have chosen to stay on this path for so long a time. But the reality is that we are on this path, and whilst we may not always understand why we have had to wait so long to find our soul mate, be encouraged that

God does understand, and if the truth be known, He not only understands, but He is also in control.

I believe there is a certain quality that is required to remain single for any given length of time, and God is confident that you and I have what it takes to go the distance. He knows that you are not going to give up or give in at this stage in your life, and He also knows that your desire is to seek Him and His Kingdom first. This statement is not a cliché with singles, but is a reality, because at the end of the day, our lives are ultimately about the King and His Kingdom.

I am confident that the woman reading this book is a person whom God can rely on and boast about regularly. You are most likely a woman who has backbone and does not need to 'see' with your natural eyes to believe the promises of God. Instead you 'see' in the spirit and know that God is controlling all events in your life to bring you to your 'wealthy place' *(Psalm 66:12)*.

Modern day society does not understand this call of God on our lives because being married or living with a partner is considered to be the norm. Therefore, most people are not able to comprehend that, even without a man, a woman in her 30s or even 40s/50s can be single and still feel fulfilled and complete within herself as a person. This creates all kinds of misconceptions regarding who we are as individuals. To be fair to them, the carnal mind will never understand the things of God. Society's reasoning concerning this whole issue is to come up with various 'labels' for singles to wear to compensate for what they consider to be abnormal. The most common of these labels are: 'left on the shelf,'' 'too fussy,' 'a spinster,' or perhaps a bit 'frigid.' And their worst conclusion, by far, is to assume that a woman who does not have a man in her life at this juncture could have unnatural tendencies, having no desire for the opposite sex. Well, how far from the truth is that notion – right singles?! I thought you'd nod your head in agreement!

In *1 Corinthians 2:14* we are encouraged that we do not have to justify ourselves to society and its views and expectations of us as singles. It reads better in the amplified version by stating, *"But the natural, non-spiritual man does not accept or welcome or admit into his heart the gifts and teachings and revelations of the Spirit of God, for they are folly (meaningless non-sense) to him; and he is incapable of knowing them [of progressively recognising, understanding, and becoming better acquainted with them] because they are spiritually discerned and estimated and appreciated." (TAB)*

So don't allow yourselves to feel condemned or guilty just because you are over a certain age and still single. It is God who orders your steps *(Psalms 37: 23)* and you are, at this particular time in your life, where He wants you to be, on the road to fulfilling your God-given destiny.

Like myself, I am sure you too are tired of the numerous comments and questions directed to you about your marital status. And since these are not questions we can answer readily, we usually just smile and embarrassingly try to avoid answering questions that we really don't need to answer in the first place. However, we should not have to feel like this. We should strive to be that whole person God has destined us to be, married or single. And it is for this very reason that I wrote this book, to encourage you to remain optimistic at such a crucial stage in your life.

Yes, there are some of us who would like to get married any time soon, and we make no pretence about it. However, we do not need to appear like depressed zombies to the outside world, roaming about looking for "anything in a pair of trousers." We can have a lot of fun in our single season. There is so much we can appreciate during this time such as travelling, meeting new people, starting a business, and much more. There are various chapters in this book covering these grounds which hopefully will give you a few ideas if you feel that you are at a loss, but somehow, I don't believe that is the case. You're too confident to be in that category. God has already revealed to me the kind of women who will be reading this book, and I pray that its contents will only enhance what God has already spoken within your spirit.

The bottom line is that there isn't much point in trying to figure out why God allows some women to get married early, for some as young as in their twenties, and He requires some to wait until their thirties or perhaps forties/fifties. However, we can confidently put our trust in God's Word, which states,

"For my thoughts are not your thoughts, neither are your ways my ways, saith the Lord. For as the heavens are higher than the earth, so are my ways higher than your ways, and my thoughts than your thoughts" (Isaiah 55:8-9 KJV).

As you allow this book to minister to you on a personal level, I want you to know that you are a special and unique woman of excellence. Regardless of your marital status, you can walk tall and be an example in your words and deeds. Your time is precious, so don't waste it by walking around looking pitiful and depressed just because you don't have a man in your life; instead, live and enjoy your life to the fullest! The depth of your relationship with God will prepare you for any future relationships you enter. And when you intimately develop your relationship with God for His highest glory, all other relationships on a human level will fall into their rightful place.

As a single woman, be encouraged by Solomon's words in the book of Ecclesiastes that to everything there is a season. In nature, no matter how cold the winter gets, it <u>cannot stay that way</u>; it has to give way for the spring to break forth. And then spring, with its fresh crispness, must give way to summer. And even the summer has to bow to the fact that autumn has its rightful place, too, and will overtake summer in due season. So as you can see, just like nature, your life too revolves around seasons. And even though some seasons might take us by surprise by staying a bit longer than we originally anticipated, we can remain focused on God and know that our circumstances will change to make room for the next season in our lives and all the challenges and opportunities that season will bring.

Andrea Best

Chapter One

LET'S BE HONEST WITH OURSELVES

"And you will know the truth, and the truth shall set you free"
– (John 8:32 KJV).

Whether we agree with the statement or not, it has been said that the first step taken in any given situation, no matter how small, will be the most crucial step to total victory. Keeping that in mind, we single women aged 30 and over need to take that first step. Regardless of how daunting it may seem, we owe it to ourselves to examine our lives with complete honesty. Part of that process will be the reality of accepting our status as mature single women, especially when we still have not found that 'special relationship' that we may have dreamt of and desired for so many years.

So let's take a closer look to see if there are any underlying issues regarding our single status. The question of whether you have had a relationship, lost one, or would like to be in one, is neither here nor there – the true facts relating to your present circumstances cannot be denied. However, don't despair; there is hope and a way forward. As we trust our entire future into God's hands, there is a foreseeable, fulfilling future ahead for us. The God that we have committed our lives to is Omnipotent, Omniscient, and Omnipresent, which translates into God being all powerful, God knowing all things, and God being everywhere simultaneously. And for the mature single woman, that thought is reassuring. It means that we can get on with our lives and not have to feel frustrated because we have not yet found our soul mate. It also means that we don't have to idly sit around feeling depressed, beating ourselves up by asking questions such as "who is he?" "Where is he going to come from?" "What does he look like?" - and all the other questions we often rehearse in our minds trying to figure things out.

The good news, however, is that we can cast all our cares upon our God. He really is concerned about every aspect of our lives and has given us permission to transfer these cares over to Him (and that includes our concerns about our marital status). If there is an issue that concerns us, then you can bet that issue will concern God too.

Therefore it is comforting to know that we do not have to deal with such complex issues in our own strength. We are encouraged by God's Word:

"Casting the whole of your care – your anxieties, all your worries, all your concerns, once and for all – on Him; for He cares for you affectionately, and cares about you watchfully"– (1 Peter 5:7 TAB).

With that promise in our favour, we do not have to worry about our marital status in the slightest bit, for we know that the God who is Almighty is on our side. And armed with the knowledge that God controls <u>all</u> situations, knows <u>all</u> things, and is <u>everywhere</u> in the world, do we really think that He is unable to orchestrate the circumstances in our lives for us to meet our soul mate? – I think not! Take comfort, my sisters, from *Jeremiah 32:17, where the prophet proclaims, "Alas, Lord God! Behold, You made the heavens and the earth by Your great power and by Your stretched out arm! There is <u>nothing too hard</u> or too wonderful for You" (TAB).*

It is unfortunate, however, that society has labelled single women over the age of 30 as being "left on the shelf," making us feel almost insecure about our singleness. It is not atypical to be alone in life at such an age, and for those of you who have reached this age and have not yet found your soul mate, please be assured that you are normal and that you are a valued member of society.

As a 'kingdom woman' you do not have to worry about being 'left on the shelf,' because God does not have any shelves in His house; be careful not to mentally erect any of your own, either. *"But in a great house there are not only vessels of gold and silver, but also of wood and of earth; and some to honour, and some to dishonour. If a man (or woman) purges himself (herself) from these, he (she) shall be a vessel unto honour, sanctified and meet for the master's use, and prepared unto every good work" (2 Timothy 2:20-21 KJV)*. If we allow ourselves to be honourable single vessels in God's house, we will be used for His highest glory and prepared unto every good work. We have all been blessed with gifts to be used in our own particular ministries; therefore, we do not have to wear the labels that society tries to place on us.

There may be all kinds of reasons why we have not found our soul mate. One reason may be that our timing is different from God's timing. And if we found our soul mate in our timing, then the right man could end up being the wrong man at that time, simply because God was not allowed to finish grooming and preparing him for us. From past experiences I have learnt that God's timing is always the best, therefore He does not have to explain or justify Himself to us in any way.

Within our waiting time we can learn so many invaluable lessons. We can learn how to develop our character, our stability, and our trust in God, all of which requires a quality of faith in Him. We can enjoy the quality time that we have with God and appreciate the wisdom He teaches us to prepare for that season in our lives when we enter into it. When we ascertain God's perfect will for our lives, we will become less fearful of the future and appreciate each new day that He gives us.

We will also acquire the virtue of patience, which allows God to give us the desires of our hearts in

His time. In the meantime, it is important that we get involved in establishing His Kingdom, allowing ourselves to be used wholly by Him. *1 Corinthians 7:32 reminds us that "The unmarried woman careth for the things that belong to the Lord, how she may please the Lord."* And whilst this thought is commendable, the truth is that there will be times when our emotions get the better of us and we wander off into our own little dream world. However, God knows our thoughts and our concerns, and He promises that if we serve Him wholeheartedly, He will reward us favourably *(Psalm 31:23)*. As Jehovah Gmolah (the God of Recompense), He is obligated to reward you for the choices you make. Rather than sitting around idly, His desire is that we get our priorities in order – by seeking Him first. And by doing so and walking in an upright way before Him, He cannot help but to give us those things that we are asking and believing Him for *(Matthew 6:33)*.

His very nature is that of one who is a giver and not a taker, neither is He a tease. He will not play around with your feelings or emotions when He knows the true desires of your heart. *Roman 10:11* encourages us that *"No man (woman in our case) who believes in Him [who adheres to, relies on, and trusts in Him] will [ever] be put to shame or be disappointed" (TAB)*. We have God's personal guarantee that *"God is not a man that He should tell or act a lie, neither the son of man, that He should feel repentance or compunction [for what He has promised]. Has He said and shall He not do it? Or has He spoken and shall He not make it good?" (Numbers 23:19 TAB)*.

Therefore, as we continue to be honest with ourselves and allow the truth of God's Word to set us free, we mentally take away any control that Satan thinks he has over us regarding our circumstances. This is because he now has no ammunition to use against us to frustrate the call of God on our lives. And without that crucial ammunition, he then has to go back to the drawing board to devise a whole new set of plans to make his counterattack. The truth of the matter is that the enemy cannot get very far when we wise up to his tactics, because his whole game is based on manipulation and deception. He is the master of deception, but God's truth counterattacks the lies that the enemy tries to use to destroy us and to hold us in bondage.

As we learn to develop our relationship with God, He in turn develops His trust in us and will start to reveal the hidden secrets of the kingdom of darkness that Satan devises for our downfall *(Isaiah 45:2-3)*. As mature Christian singles, it is imperative that we put on the whole armour of God, because it is this armour that will protect us from the wiles of the devil *(Ephesians 6:10-17)*. Putting on parts of the armour will not enable us to be effective against the enemy. However, putting on the **whole** spiritual coat of armour will equip us for the spiritual warfare that all Christians must engage in, whether we are single or married.

Verse 14 of Ephesians 6 urges us to walk in the truth. *"Stand therefore [hold your ground], having tightened the belt of truth around your loins and having put on the breastplate of integrity and of moral rectitude and right standing with God" (TAB).* As mature singles who are called into battle, we are going to have to know how to stand and hold our ground, because Satan will, from time to time, use our single status to be the brunt of jokes which could cause us to take our eyes and focus off God for a brief moment. However, when we allow God's truth to envelope us, we will at all times be able to differentiate between the enemy's lies as opposed to God's truth. Isaiah asked the question, *"Who has believed (trusted in, relied upon, and clung to) our message?" (Isaiah 53:1 TAB).* And today the Holy Spirit directs that same question back to us – "Whose report will we believe?" Whose version of events will we trust in, rely on, and cling to?

Regardless of what we go through, God's truth is to be the final authority in our lives. That same truth will keep and preserve us throughout the challenges we will face as mature singles *(Psalm 40:11).* As Christians, God's truth should be a trait that is imbedded deep within our hearts. David knew this only too well when he wrote, *"Behold, you desire truth in the inner being; make me therefore to know wisdom in my inmost heart" (–Psalm 51:6 TAB).* This inner cleansing came about after David honestly admitted to God that he had failed miserably by having an affair with a married woman, and that he had devised a plan to have her husband killed when he had learnt that she was pregnant with his child. However, after he had come clean and was honest with God, the enemy had nothing to condemn him with. The Message translation of *Psalm 51:6-7 records David's confession like this: "What you're after is truth from the inside out. Enter me, then; conceive a new, true life. Soak me in your laundry and I'll come out clean, scrub me and I'll have a snow-white life" (TM).*

Now that you have cleared that first crucial hurdle and come to terms with your single status, the next chapter will show you how unique you are as a woman of God. It will also show you how God has designed every step of your life, and that no area of your life is an accident or surprise to Him. You will realise that you were born with a specific purpose in life – to be *you*.

CHAPTER TWO

YOU ARE UNIQUE!
YOU WERE BORN TO BE YOU

"Oh yes, you shaped me first inside, then out; you formed me in my mother's womb. I thank you, High God – you're breathtaking! Body and soul, I am marvellously made! I worship in adoration – <u>what a creation</u>! You know me inside and out, you know every bone in my body; you know exactly how I was made, bit by bit, how I was <u>sculpted from nothing into something</u>. Like an open book, you watched me <u>grow from conception to birth</u>; all the stages of my life were spread out before you, the days of my life all prepared before I'd even lived one day"
(Psalm 139: 13-16 TM)

Contrary to popular belief and the Darwin theory, the good news is that human beings did not evolve from apes. Neither are we descendants of the chimpanzee and gorilla species, as intimated by scientific theories written in the nineteenth century that questioned the biblical account of creation. However, it is clear from David's account in Psalm 139 that we were personally created with much intricate detail by the Omnipotent Creator, the Almighty God Himself.

As individuals, we are so unique that our frame was not hid from God when we were being formed in secret and intricately and curiously wrought in the depths of the earth. This view would, therefore, rule out the pro-choice argument that a foetus is of no value and has no life when discussing the woman's right to have an abortion. Our entrance into planet earth begins in an embryonic stage, and by week eight of our development, all of our major organs have been formed and continue to grow at a very fast rate. So much so that by the twentieth week the foetus may already have eyebrows and fingernails [1]. *Psalms 139:16 confirms this truth: "Thine eyes did see my substance, yet being unperfect; and in thy book <u>all my members were written</u>, which in continuance were fashioned, when as yet there was none of them" (KJV).* Therefore, it is very clear that from inception we are designed and formed with a specific purpose.

If knowledge of such magnitude is not enough to convince you of how valuable you are to the heavenly Father, think of the race involved before the moment of conception when thousands of sperm travel in the womb to come in contact with one egg, a race for life itself. **You** did not just happen by chance, but **you** were ordained by God to be a part of His creation, imbued by Him with your own unique characteristics, gifts, and talents. Apart from multiple births, one egg out of 500,000 and one sperm out of 200,000[2] join to form *you* – now that's unique! Therefore, as a mature single woman, I want you to know that you are unique and very special to God. He values you regardless of your marital status.

Now that you have seen how unique you are, quit trying to be somebody else and instead concentrate on being the best person you can be. You would make a lousy somebody else, because you were made to be you. *"For I know the plans I have for **you** declares the Lord, plans to prosper **you** and not to harm **you**, plans to give **you** hope and a future" (Jeremiah 29:11 NIV).*

You are special and valuable in the sight of God. You were born with a specific purpose in life and only you can fulfil that destiny; therefore put your entire trust in God who desires for you to be the person that He has predestined you to be. *Romans 8: 29-30 (TM)* reveals that *"God knew what He was doing from the very beginning. He decided from the outset to shape the lives of those who would love Him along the same lines as the life of His Son. The Son stands first in the line of humanity He restored. We see the original and intended shape of our lives there in Him. After God made the decision of what His children should be like, He followed it up by calling people by name. After He called them by name, He set them on a solid basis with Himself. And then, after getting them established, He stayed with them to the end, gloriously completing what He had begun."*

Pause for a moment and imagine that you could be any person in the whole world (past and present) — who would you be? (Think about this for a while!) I often asked myself this question when I was a young child growing up and now that I am a mature adult, the answer has not changed over the years – I still come back to one person, and that person is me. Despite all the personal trials I have encountered, including attacks to my self esteem concerning my outward appearance at specific times in my life, I can honestly say that there has never been a moment when I had wished I was somebody else, because I have always liked and enjoyed being myself. However, that does not mean that there have not been people I've admired growing up, because there have been. I believe Halle Berry to be incredibly beautiful, but I have never wanted to be her. Regardless of how stunning she may appear on our screens, I'm sure Halle has her own personal problems to contend with. From an early age, God instilled within me a sense of personal worth that I was to have for myself as well as for other individuals, in that all individuals are special, unique, and possess great qualities within themselves to be the very best that they can be.

Apart from God, you are the only one who truly knows you intimately, and when we try to be somebody else, it is an insult to the Creator of His workmanship, since He created us with such detail and precision. *Ephesians 2:10 (TAB)* reminds us, *"For we are God's [own] handiwork (His workmanship), recreated in Christ Jesus, [born anew] that we may do those good works which God predestined (planned beforehand) for us [taking paths which He prepared ahead of time], that we should walk in them [living the good life which He prearranged for and made ready for us to live].*

Another person's beauty can be desirable, and yet another person's talents may be something to be emulated, but to "walk in someone else's shoes" is to take on **all** their emotional, physical, and spiritual characteristics and any other "baggage" that they might be carrying. On the face of it, it would appear far easier to be ourselves, particularly because we have spent a lifetime growing and developing our individual characters, and as a unique person, we should be celebrated, for we are extraordinary beings in our own individual way. Therefore, be comfortable with yourself, your character, and your looks. Always remember that God thinks that you are special, so much so that He has ingrained your personal name into the palms of His hands. Every day when He looks at His hands, pierced with the reminder that He died for you, He can't fail to have you in His thoughts, and that's unique.

"Behold, I have indelibly imprinted (tattooed) a picture of you on the palm of each of My hands, O Zion, your walls are continually before Me" (Isaiah 49:16 TAB). Never think that you are unimportant to God, because that simply is not true. The way God has designed our frame is astonishing, and it should really bring to our minds what an awesome God we have "batting on our side." We are guaranteed to win every time. However, not everyone is confident about who they are. There are many

people who have no self-worth and do not value themselves as important and unique. And it is these people whose self-esteem is sometimes so low that they attempt to take their own lives, because they fail to recognise the potential that is within them. However, God extends His arms of love to embrace all who will receive His love.

Imagine the scenario of a rubbish heap. Picture the many items now discarded because people no longer have use for them. But don't be so quick to walk away; take a closer look — perhaps you can find something that can be useful again. For many of us, our lives were like rubbish heaps before we became a Christian. People had given up on us and declared that we were not fit for anything and so therefore had discarded us. However, God saw beauty amongst our debris, offering us hope and a way out in the person of His Son Jesus. He looked beyond our faults and saw far into our unique future. *Romans 5:6 (TAB)* shows us what God thought of us well before we even knew who He was, and these verses reassure us how He did not forsake us, but instead accepted us. *"While we were yet in weakness [powerless to help ourselves], at the fitting time Christ died for (in behalf of) the ungodly."*

So as you reflect on your uniqueness and contemplate on your single status, take time to glance at the following scriptures; this will give you an indication of how special you are to God. They are filled with truth and revelation that God had a call on your life long before you ever existed, even before your parents came together. Wow, what a God! Now that alone should blow your mind.

Psalm 139; Jeremiah 1:4-5; Romans 8:29-30; Ephesians 1:4-5, 11; Ephesians 2:10.

Chapter Three

ALONE BUT NOT LONELY

As believers, God has assured us, "I'll never let you down, never walk off and leave you" (Hebrews 13:5 [latter] TM).

From the previous chapters we have learnt to honestly come to terms with our single status. We have also learnt that we are unique and special to God. But as mature single women we inevitably will experience seasons of loneliness.

In this chapter we will explore how this alone time can be used effectively to develop our relationship with God. *James 4:8 (TAB)* urges us to *"Come close to God and He will come close to you."* Verse 10 encourages, *"Humble yourself – feeling very insignificant – in the presence of the Lord, and He will exalt you. He will lift you up and make your life significant."* I believe there is a specific, God-given reason why you have been led down the path that you are now on. It is not a mistake; likewise, God did not arbitrarily choose to bless others with husbands and leave you out. Therefore, you can draw tremendous strength by trusting God in every area of your life and not leaning on your own understanding. In all your ways acknowledge Him, and He will direct your paths *(see Proverb 3:5-6).*

You do not have to live life feeling depressed, downtrodden, or miserable. Instead, you can make the choice to have a positive attitude, choosing to be happy and enjoying the unique lifestyle that God has blessed you with. You may have already purchased your own property and live on your own, but you do not have to feel lonely in these circumstances, because God has promised that He will never leave or abandon you. That means He will always be there; He can be relied upon and He can be trusted. In your time of need, He will be there to comfort and protect you. This is a great time in your life for developing your character and independence as a mature single woman, whilst remaining totally dependent on God.

Personally, I always imagined that I would have left the parental home on the "arms of a man," but for me it didn't happen that way, and you too may have a similar story to mine. I eventually left home at the age of 29, having felt the need to establish myself in the great, big world if only to prove to myself that I could make it and enjoy life in my current single status. Also, I wanted to discover if I could find true fulfilment within myself and in my relationship with

God. Fourteen years later, I have not regretted taking that first daunting step, and I thoroughly enjoy living on my own. It does help, though, if you enjoy your own company, because if you can't be happy in your own company, what man deserves to be subjected to your mood swings and unhappiness?

Throughout this time I have learnt to develop and deepen my walk with God. I can honestly say that I do not experience bouts of loneliness on a regular basis. (However, one does have the occasional "pity party," which always seems to coincide with "the time of the month," so I'll just blame it on the hormones!) I also know that I could not have reached this stage in my life without the support of my family, friends, and the fellowship of other believers in my local church, all of whom have contributed to me being a sound and wholesome individual. That is how important a network of people are for the mature single, so don't ostracise yourself from people, but instead embrace and appreciate their input in your life.

I have been blessed with a large and close-knit family. For as long as I can remember, we have always gathered as a family on numerous occasions, whether it be just sitting around having a laugh, going on outings, gathering for holidays, and so on. I get to experience the best of both worlds: enjoying their company, and also appreciating the fact that I can go back home to my "pad" and enjoy my own quiet solitude once again. Over the years these times of fellowship have played a great part in fighting the loneliness factor of living on my own.

Also, being involved in a good, strong, local church has its rewards. Getting involved and staying active prevents loneliness and boredom from settling in permanently. Try making friendships with a view to developing lasting relationships, because the people whom God allows to come into your life will be a great asset to you if you ever need a shoulder to cry on or you need someone to talk to or pray with. Sometimes my flat appears to be a place where I go just to lay my head. I'm in and out constantly. All I seem to do is drop things off and pick things up. There are times when I wonder if I really live there.

Also as a mature single your life can be used for the glory of God to be a role model to those younger singles who are watching your every move and aspiring to be like you. What message will you send them? Will it be the message of a frustrated spinster who is sitting around waiting to get married in order to "begin life," or will it be the message of a well-balanced woman who knows her mind and is in tune with the leading of the Holy Spirit?

It is important that you enjoy your singleness, whether you live on your own, share a flat with other girlfriends, or live with your parents. Don't wish your life away for something that might not happen; there is a big world out there waiting to be explored. Just think of your singleness as unique. Not every woman has the ability to stay single for a great length of time. God knew whom He could entrust with this walk. And you are the person I am referring to — someone who was drawn to the title of this book on the shelf in the bookshop and who could identify with it. God knows your personal characteristics. Of course, desiring to be married will be an issue that comes up from time to time, but He knows that you are mature enough to handle it. *1 Corinthians 10:13* tells us that God will not allow us to be tempted beyond what we can bear. Therefore, a good key to evaluating your situation is that if God allows you to go through something, then this means He has confidence that you are able to come through it triumphantly – with flying colours *(Hebrews 10:35)*.

You may be fully aware that God has asked you to remain single for a period of time, but rest assured you don't have to feel lonely or despondent. God will always meet you at your point of need. In *1 Kings 17:1*, God made provision for Elijah by way of sending ravens to feed him at the brook Cherith. This brook was the exact spot where God required Elijah to be at this particular point in his life and was where Elijah would be strengthened. In our own unique circumstances, God too will meet us at our particular well or brook and make provisions for us. The well/brook may be our local church, a daily devotional we read, or a radio or television ministry we regularly listen to. If there is an avenue that we habitually turn to on a consistent basis, God will use this outlet to speak to us and to reveal revelations He desires us to know. In *John 4:5-26* we read the story of the Samaritan woman who came regularly to the well to get water. Jesus met her at this 'well' and provided something that would change her life forever – the living water of choosing eternal life through salvation. When God deposits a *rhema* word in our lives as a result of Him meeting us at our brook/well, our lives are never the same from that moment forward. Your single status is your brook/well. It is at this place that God will consistently fill you with the knowledge of His Word, which will enable you to be strengthened throughout this time whilst you are alone. It's a time for you to be still and know that He is God. He will not be rushed in ordering your steps towards meeting your soul mate. All He asks is that you trust Him and feel secure in His presence, because He has promised not to let you down or walk off and leave you *(Hebrews 13:5)*.

In summary, we have learned in this chapter how it is possible to be alone without being lonely. Most importantly, we have our relationship with God, our family, and our friends to draw on. In the next chapter we will see how the mature single woman has the opportunity to fulfil some of her life-long goals and the many exciting things that she can get involved with. So, as you can see, woman of God, you cannot afford to sit at home feeling sorry for yourself; there is so much to live and be grateful for as we remain active and vibrant for His highest glory.

Chapter Four

LIVE YOUR LIFE "IN THE NOW"

"I call heaven and earth to witness this day against you, that I have set before you life and death, the blessing and the curse, therefore <u>choose life</u>, that you and your descendants <u>may live</u>"
(Deuteronomy 30:19 TAB).

So far we have learned that we have so much going for us as mature single women. However, at times we can make the mistake of dwelling in the past or dreaming about the future to such an extent that we fail to realise the actual season of our lives that we are living in. And though it is good to have goals and dreams to attain to, we must not disregard our present state.

God has given us the choice of life or death; this can be expanded to mean we have the choice to live life to the fullest right now, or we can walk around as if we are dead (having no zest for life in us). And just in case we might need a bit of help making up our mind, He gives us a little nudge in the right direction, which is to "choose life." Life is for living, so don't be afraid to make the most of it. Satan is the number one enemy of our joy. Like a thief, he comes to steal, kill, and destroy us, but Jesus came to give us life as well as our eternal future, enabling us to greet each day with a sense of expectancy and fulfilment. *"The thief comes only in order to steal and kill and destroy. I came that they may have and enjoy life, and have it in abundance (to the full, till it overflows)" (John 10:10 TAB)*.

Singles, I challenge you to try a different approach. Wake up every morning with the attitude that you are going to have a great day. It's your choice and you can will it into your life. Learn to appreciate the beauty of nature that God has given us to enjoy. There is so much to do and see. Even though we might not get to see or experience everything in our lifetime, we can still choose to make a start and give it our best shot.

How about travelling abroad and seeing various places? Learn the joy of experiencing and embracing other cultures. It has only been in the last ten years that I have realised the importance of taking time out, setting apart a special time for myself to enjoy a holiday. I really enjoy getting on an aeroplane and jetting off to the unknown, because I do not know what I am going to find when I get there, so it is a bit like a lucky dip. You can be pleasantly surprised by the various people you meet, their way of life, the cuisine, and the general feel of the place. It also helps if you have good company when travelling, and I am very fortunate that my younger sister, Shelly, has the same interests in travelling as I have, which makes it great fun.

Together we have visited places such as Barbados, the homeland of our parents; Florida because we are big kids and we adore Mickey & Minnie Mouse; the Bahamas, Euro Disney and we have had holidays in the United Kingdom where other family members have joined in such as at Center Parcs, which was great fun. In the last two to three years we have been to Toronto, Portugal, Brussels, and Barcelona, and in May 2005 we went to St Lucia. And it doesn't stop there. This year (2006) we are off to Tenerife and are thinking about taking a cruise in a couple of years.

Are you beginning to get the picture? You don't have to put your life on hold in your wait for "Mr. Right" – so get out there and start enjoying yourself and seeing new places (spend some money and invest in yourself). Your "Mr. Right" is more likely to appreciate a woman with some experience and interest to her credit than someone with no substance whose only aspiration has been to put her life on hold so as to cater to his every whim.

Also, God has given you this time to yourself, so use it wisely and pursue your hobbies. Think of what you are genuinely passionate about, because this is most likely where you will discover your God-given gifts and destiny. Perhaps you have always wanted to learn a new language. Well, you are never going to be fluent in French, German, or any other language until you take that first step and sign up for some classes.

Or maybe you dabble a bit in sewing for yourself or for a few close friends. Dress designing could be the avenue that will make you your millions. Therefore, do something about it and pursue your passions and those things that you get pleasure from. From a very young age I was always interested in reading books and writing. I can vividly remember when I was at junior school we had a mobile library which I visited regularly to take books home to read. That's where my passion for reading began. I have always expressed my thoughts by writing things down, but it has only been in the last eight years that I have actually come to terms with the fact that I am fulfilled when I write. Therefore, I decided to act on my desires and I took an evening course in freelance journalism, which gave me the relevant skills and know-how to succeed, and the rest is history.

My sister Shelly is extremely creative, and recently she began making greeting cards, which then developed into her designing and making wedding invitations, business cards, and other stationery-type products. She is kept very busy by the orders she is receiving, and she fits the criteria of the mature single woman that I have been referring to. Shelly is doing something positive with her time and energy by making her talent and interests work for her, and I believe you can too.

One other point in utilising the time you have now as a mature single is to make yourself accessible, not only to God and your family, but also to others. Try to develop new relationships. *"A man that hath friends must show himself friendly: and there is a friend that sticketh closer than a brother" (Proverbs 18:24 KJV)*. God will also give you favour when it comes to developing friendships. People will be drawn to you, desiring to network with you. *"Thus says the Lord of hosts: In those days ten men out of all languages of the nations shall take hold of the robe of him who is a Jew, saying, let us go with you, for we have heard that God is with you" (Zechariah 8:23 TAB)*. Just think, a smile may cost nothing for you to give, but it might mean the world to someone in need of it. Therefore, ask God to show you the people He wants you to minister to, and do not let that window of opportunity pass you by. Make yourself available now, whilst you have so much free time, and be a blessing to God and His kingdom.

If you've ever seen the film "Dead Poet's Society" with Robin Williams[1] you'll know it's based on the story of a teacher who inspires his pupils to live life to the fullest. He encourages them to live by the motto of *Carpe Diem*, which is Latin for "seize the day." Paul challenges us with these very same words in *Ephesians 5:15-16: "Look carefully then how you walk! Live purposefully and worthily and accurately, not as the unwise and witless, but as wise (sensible, intelligent people), making the very most of the time [buying up each opportunity], because the days are evil" (TAB)*. As I said before, as mature singles we cannot afford to dwell on the past or be dreamy-eyed about the future; instead we have to make the most of every opportunity. Marriage may be something we want in our future, but our lives could be taken away from us at an early age. None of us knows what our future holds, and therefore we should value each day we are given and live it to the best of our knowledge and ability.

The book of James endorses this fact in *James 4:13-15: "Come now, you who say, today or tomorrow we will go into such and such a city and spend a year there and carry on our business and make money. Yet you do not know [the least thing] about what may happen tomorrow. What is the nature of your life? You are [really] but a wisp of vapour (a puff of smoke, a mist) that is visible for a little while and then disappears [into thin air]. You ought instead to say, if the Lord is willing, we shall live and we shall do this or that [thing]" (TAB)*.

Moments passed will never return. God's time of visitation is now – don't let it pass you by; these times are often your windows of opportunity. So whilst you have breath in your lungs, let *Carpe Diem* be your motto. Go ahead and seize your moments - live life to the fullest. Live it **now!**

CHAPTER FIVE

DON'T STAY B*I*TTER – GET B*E*TTER

"Weeping may endure for <u>a night</u>, but joy cometh in the morning" (Psalm 30:5 TAB) – The same verse in <u>The Message</u> translation reads "The nights of crying your eyes out give way to <u>days of laughter.</u>"

It's probably a chapter in your life that you would prefer to sweep under the carpet and leave somewhere in a heap without ever having to deal with it. But you and I both know that the pile will always be there as a constant reminder, and it will continue to irritate you until you do something about it.

It is fair to say that most women have been hurt at one time or another, at some stage in their lives. However, it is how we deal with the hurts of the past that will determine our future relationships. If you really, really want to dump that emotional baggage out of your life, you need to take that first initial step, which is to **get over it**. This may sound harsh, and you may think I am being cold and callous, but it is the only way you're going to get on with the rest of your life. You cannot afford to go on day after day replaying those scenes over and over in your mind. Doing so will destroy you and cause you to be an emotional wreck, which of course is the plan of the enemy — to keep you bound and tied to the past for as long as he can. You mean nothing to him, and he is not in the least bit interested in any aspect of your life, but God is and He cares about you and your future well-being. It is for this reason why He continually requests that His children adopt a spirit of forgiveness when they are abused, betrayed, and treated unfairly.

If you are one of those individuals who continues to be indignant, wanting to hang on to the hurt, not willing to forgive, then the Bible says that God doesn't hear your prayers when you come to Him for forgiveness. In *Matthew 6:14-15 (TAB)* this is made clear by Jesus to His disciples when He says, *"For if you forgive people their trespasses [their reckless and wilful sins, leaving them, letting them go, and giving up resentment], your heavenly Father will also forgive you. But if you do not forgive others their trespasses [their reckless and wilful sins, leaving them, letting them go, and giving up resentment], neither will your Father forgive you your trespasses."* So, as you can see, holding unforgiveness in your heart against another person jeopardises your own personal relationship with God. In *Matthew 5:23-24 (TAB)*, Jesus says that before you present your gifts to God you should check your heart to see if you are holding resentment against another, and if you are, you are to deal with it before you make your petitions to Him. *"So if when you are offering your gift at the altar you there remember that your brother has any [grievance] against you, leave your gift at the altar and go. First make peace with your brother, and then come back and present your gift."*

I appreciate the fact that you might not be able to confront the individual in person, as it may be that they had left on bad terms or perhaps for reasons unique to your situation. Nevertheless, you can release those hurts to God and allow Him to heal your inner person, whilst allowing Him to soothe and comfort your soul. The healing will begin to take place as you allow His Word to minister unto you. *"Do not let your hearts be troubled (distressed, agitated). You believe in and adhere to and trust in and rely on God; believe in and adhere to and trust in and rely also on Me" (John 14:1 TAB)*. Therefore, if Jesus doesn't want you to be agitated and distressed, why would you continue to live in such a state? Jesus offers you His peace which is so different from anything you have ever experienced before, so why would you throw that away in exchange for turmoil? Jesus instructs us in *John 14: 27 (TAB)*, *"Peace I leave with you; My [own] peace I now give and bequeath to you. Not as the world gives do I give to you. Do not let your hearts be troubled, neither let them be afraid. [Stop allowing yourself to be agitated and disturbed; and do not permit yourselves to be fearful and intimidated and cowardly and unsettled]."*

If you are nursing a broken heart, you need to thank God that you are out of the relationship that caused it to break. Yeah, you heard me right! Praise God! Did you ever stop to think that the reason you might have broken up with that man was because God knew he wasn't the right one for you in the first place? Staying in that relationship possibly would have taken you down the wrong route contrary to the destiny God has planned for you. "Mr. Wrong's" **loss** will be "Mr. Right's" **gain,** so never be too upset when a man decides he wants to leave. Let him go with your blessing, even though emotionally that is easier said than done. We should not hold onto anything too tightly, because we never know when God might ask us to give it up. If your life was wrapped up in this individual to the point where you didn't know what would become of your life if he were to leave, then girlfriend, he **definitely** needed to go. The only person you are to be solely dependent upon is God – and God alone.

Yes, you may have taken a knock in terms of your self-worth or self-esteem, but you don't have to remain there. *Psalm 92:12* gives us hope: *"The righteous will flourish like the palm tree."* It is said that a palm tree can withstand any storm that comes against it. It may bend and sway, but it won't go down, because its roots are imbedded deep into its foundation. As a mature Christian single, what foundation are you rooted in? *2 Corinthians 4:8-9* also encourages that *"We are hedged in (pressed) on every side [troubled and oppressed in every way], but not cramped or crushed; we suffer embarrassments and are perplexed and unable to find a way out, but not driven to despair; we are pursued (persecuted and hard driven), but not deserted [to stand alone]; we are struck down to the ground, but never struck out and destroyed" (TAB)*. No matter how severe the break-up was, and even though there will be questions in your mind about the relationship that will possibly never get answered (to your satisfaction anyway), don't allow bitterness to take root in your heart, because there is hope ... and with God, **the future is always bright.**

Let me assure you that when you decide to give up the hurt and forgive the individual(s), you will get another opportunity to love again. Guess what? That man isn't the only guy on the planet. And when you take a step back and see where your last relationship went wrong, you will be able to clearly see the mistakes you made along the way. I say "clearly." because when we are so in love, walking around with our head in the clouds, we sometimes ignore and excuse the little faults that perhaps annoy us and that God has been trying to show us, but we have refused to pay attention to. And before you venture into that next relationship, get closure on the previous one and then ask God to guide you. Ask Him to direct your path to the right person so that you will be absolutely convinced in your heart that he is the right man for you.

As a woman, I believe in waiting to be asked out without having to chase or hunt the man down. Yes, I know we are living in the 21st century and that many people seem to have varying views on this subject, but my personal view is that I wouldn't want to appear desperate to a potential mate. Men are known to be hunters, and whilst at times it may seem flattering to them when they are being chased, deep down I believe that they would prefer to do the hunting rather than be the hunted. Ladies, let them do their jobs!

Furthermore, if I did the chasing, then what does that say about my faith in God? Am I so desperate and impatient to wait for God to lead the right man to me that I feel I have to help Him along? I believe that our inability to wait on God has led us to the wrong men, and that through this impatience we have brought pain into our lives unnecessarily. *"Lean on, trust in, and be confident in the Lord with all your heart and mind and <u>do not rely on your own insight or understanding</u>. In all your ways know, recognise, and acknowledge Him, and He will direct and make straight and plain your paths" (Proverbs 3:6-7 TAB).* The Bible could not have made it any clearer— we are to lean His way rather than relying on our own insight. In return, He will direct us and make straight (or clear) our paths (the route we are to take). To add even more weight to this truth, verse 7 states *"Be not wise in your own eyes; reverently fear and worship the Lord and turn [entirely] away from evil."*

Being wise in our own eyes could tempt us to date an individual who does not have a born-again relationship with Jesus Christ. We might reason to ourselves that there are no men in the church our age, and so we decide to take up the offer of the unsaved men who appears to have it going on. But ladies, can we really fool ourselves so easily? You're a wise, godly woman, one who has her head on mature shoulders; let's be honest — how can a man who has not submitted his life to God and is on his way to a Christ-less eternity, really have it 'going on?' And what can he tell you about living a godly life, especially when you know that the true source of life can only be found in having a relationship with Jesus Christ? This is just another one of those lies that Satan whispers in our ears at those vulnerable times in our lives. This is part of his master plan — to throw us off course and off the path that God has designed for us. At all times we have to know who God is and what His will is for our lives. When we know the voice and ways of God, we will recognise the counterfeit men, the "wolves in sheep's clothing" that will come along.

Over the years I've heard some unsaved men remark that when they're eventually ready to settle down, they're heading straight to the church to find "a good wife." And their logic behind this reasoning is that they do not want to change their lifestyle, but a "good Christian woman" would treat them well and put up with their behaviour because of her godly and meek nature. Ladies, you see what kind of "wolves" we are up against! However, I know that such men will not be able to deceive any woman of excellence who is reading this book, because to be forewarned is to be forearmed. And God has equipped us with the truth of His Word so that we do not allow ourselves to be distracted or deceived.

Ladies, remember — just because we are meek does not mean that we are weak. Growing up in the church, I used to hear preachers talk against marrying unsaved men, and I used to feel that perhaps they were being a bit harsh and that it was up to the individual to personally make that decision. However, after experiencing a relationship with an unsaved man (and I'm glad to say it only took one such relationship to bring me to my senses), my views have changed drastically, and I now believe those preachers to be correct in what they teach. We should not dismiss their counsel but instead take heed to it.

At a church I attended, the pastors often taught from the pulpit on the dos and don'ts concerning dating and developing relationships. They always stressed the dangers in dating unsaved men. And even though they showed us from the Word of God all the correct reasoning behind why it was not a wise decision to make, they knew that some would still believe that they could make it work for them and just go ahead and choose such a route anyway, ignoring the warning signals that God was giving to them. They also knew that those same women would eventually be back in their office to be counselled on how to save that ill-fated marriage.

Therefore, I know that what I am going to share may not go down well with some individuals, but it will save us from experiencing bitter relationships when we can wait and receive God's best. The scripture in *2 Corinthians 6:15-16 (TAB)* makes it quite plain: *"Do not be unequally yoked with believers [do not make mismated alliances with them or come under a different yoke with them, <u>inconsistent with your faith</u>]. For what partnership have right living and right standing with God with iniquity and lawlessness? Or how can light have fellowship with darkness? What harmony can there be between Christ and Belial [the devil]? <u>Or what has a believer in common with an unbeliever?</u>"* Here is the same scripture as it reads in The Message translation: *"<u>Don't become partners with those who reject God</u>. How can you make partnership out of right and wrong? That's not partnership; that's war. Is light best friends with dark? <u>Does Christ go strolling with the devil?</u> Do trust and mistrust hold hands?"* [See Chapter 10, "Square Pegs Don't Fit Into Round Holes" for more about being unequally yoked in marriage.]

At a church I attended, the pastor would quote from the Bible and sometimes say, "Tell your neighbour he didn't write that; God wrote it!" I'm also telling you that I did not write the above statement — it came from God's Word, and it is powerful and worth taking note of. Therefore, ladies, let's pay attention and take heed to the Word of God and be mindful of the teaching we receive from those who watch over our souls.

By no means is God trying to cramp our style; rather, He is trying to protect us from making wrong decisions that will affect our lives and cause us pain.

Remember that this chapter is about not staying bitter, but instead getting better. If we get our relationships right at the outset, then we will save ourselves a lot of unnecessary heartache. Woman of God, He desires for you to have the best, but in the meantime, He will teach you how He longs to be your one and only true love and how to develop true intimacy with Him.

CHAPTER SIX

GOD LONGS TO BE YOUR ONE AND ONLY TRUE LOVE

"Yes, I have loved you with an everlasting love; therefore with loving kindness have I drawn you and have continued my faithfulness to you" (Jeremiah 31:3 TAB).

The previous chapter dealt with how we are to move on from past relationships by becoming better individuals and not remaining bitter and emotionally scarred. This chapter will acquaint you with the one love that you are to give your earnest desires and attention to as a mature single. If you don't already know, I want to let you know that you will never, ever receive from another human being the kind of love that you will receive from Almighty God. You will never have anyone love you as passionately as the way God loves you. He loves you with a selfless love, which translates in the Greek language as *agape* love. *Jeremiah 31:3* reveals the depths of God's love for us – it is everlasting. He will never at any point in our lifetime stop loving us, and when we are in despair as to finding that special love of our life, He longs to be our one and only true love. God loves us so much that even when mankind's sin separated him from God, He already had a plan in place for our redemption. *"This is how much God loved the world: He gave His son, His one and only son. And this is why: so that no one need be destroyed; by believing in Him, anyone can have a whole and lasting time" (John 3:16 TM).*

God's love for us is pure with no hidden agendas. He first loved us even with the knowledge that not everyone would return His love. *"But God shows and clearly proves His (own) love for us by the fact that while we were still sinners Christ, The Messiah, The Anointed One, died for us" (Romans 5:8 TAB).*

Perhaps some of your previous relationships may have been utterly disappointing, leaving you in a state of despair; however, God longs to show you true love, which can only be found in Him. According to *1 Corinthians Chapter 13*, God's love endures long and is patient and kind. It does not rejoice at injustice and unrighteousness, but rejoices when right and truth prevail. God's love never fails, unlike others whose love for you has failed. God's love for you never fades out, becomes obsolete, or comes to an end. His love can be trusted; **it will never let you down.** God is also looking for you to deepen your relationship with Him, because if you cannot love and be intimate with God firstly, in sincerity and honour to Him, then you will find it difficult to wholly love and be intimate with your future mate.

God wants your undivided love. He wants you to love Him with all your being, with the innermost part of your soul. We are taught this in the Ten Commandments, being the first and most important commandment. *"And He replied to him, You shall love the Lord your God with <u>all your heart</u> and with <u>all your soul</u> and with <u>all your mind</u> (intellect). This is the great (most important, principal) and first commandment" (Matthew 22:37-38 TAB).* When we learn to love God to such depths as this, we will find it easier to love our neighbour. The book of 1 John 4 beautifully portrays the source of love. *Verses 7-11 state, "Beloved, let us love one another: for love is of God; and every one that loveth is born of God, and knoweth God. He that loveth not knoweth not God; for God is love. In this was manifested the love of God toward us, because that God sent His only begotten Son into the world, that we might live through Him. <u>Herein is love, not that we loved God, but that He loved us</u>, and sent His Son to be the propitiation for our sins. Beloved, if God so loved us, we ought also to love one another." (KJV)*

There you have it; the source of how we can love God ultimately and sacrificially. He loved us first, even at a time when we were unlovely. He sees our future and knows our end. He knows what the final outcome of our lives will be and continues to lavish His love upon us even when we don't always deserve it. *Verses 18 and 19* continue to reveal, *"There is no fear in love; but perfect love casteth out fear: because fear hath torment. He that feareth is not made perfect in love. We love Him, because He first loved us." (KJV)*

We don't have to be afraid of God's love, because it is perfect already. It may be that you have been involved in a relationship in the past where your love was abused and that love turned to a fear of the person. However, you can rest assured that the love God loves you with is designed to give you peace and security. You can feel secure in His love because He cares for you and always has your best interests at heart.

Being mature single women, it is normal that feelings will surface of desiring someone to love and settle down with. For some of you this might be a great ordeal, and you are unable to shake off the constant reminders of being alone; however, be comforted in the fact that we have God to love intimately, and when all else fails, He will always be there. He understands how we feel and what we are going through, which is why He has promised to be our husband if we will allow Him to be. In all reality, you could not want for a better husband than God Himself. *"For your Maker is your Husband – the Lord of hosts is His name – and the Holy One of Israel is your Redeemer; the God of the whole earth He is called. For the Lord has called you like a woman forsaken, grieved in spirit, and heartsore – even a wife (wooed and won) in youth, when she is [later] refused and scorned says your God" (Isaiah 54:5-6 TAB).*

Don't ever allow your thinking to be contaminated by the devil's lies "that you are not special to God," because you are, and this verse proves it. When others forsake you, He will pick you up. He sees the bigger picture; He is able to see your worth, your value, and the outcome of what your future will be. *"Be satisfied with your present [circumstances and with what you have]; for He [God] Himself has said, I will not in any way fail you nor give you up nor leave you without support. [I will] not, [I will] not, [I will] not in any degree leave you helpless nor forsake nor let [you] down (relax My hold on you)! [Assuredly not!]" (Romans 13:5 TAB)*. Doesn't that sound like someone who thinks the world of you? It almost reads like a love letter, with the writer doing his utmost to assure the recipient that he will do all he can to never let her down. That love letter has each of our names on it, because it was written to us personally by the lover of our souls.

Ladies, God will also on a daily basis whisper sweet words in our ears in an intimate way – these whispers are *Rhemas* from His Word which minister to us specifically and personally in our lives. You may not have a man to whisper in your ear at those times when you feel down and need that gentle touch, but God is so much better than that physical touch, and He ministers much deeper in your soul than a man could ever do. And as He is whispering to your spirit, you will find yourself smiling knowingly – because ah! ... yes.., the lover of your soul has done it again; He has soothed your aching heart and wooed your soul. God will always have a Word for every occasion for our lives – He is faithful and we can always count on Him.

True love is selfless, and God is the only one who can ever love you like that. The love Christ has for the church is the standard that we can expect our future husbands to love us with. *"Husband, love your wives, as Christ loved the Church and gave Himself up for her" (Ephesians 5:25 TAB). Verses 28-29 go on to* state, *"Even so husbands should love their wives as [being in a sense] their own bodies. He who loves his own wife loves himself. For no man ever hated his own flesh, but nourishes and carefully protects and cherishes it, as Christ does the church." Verse 33* finally says, *"However, let each man of you [without exception] love his wife as [being in a sense] his very own self; and let the wife see that she respects and reverences her husband [that she notices him, regards him, honors him, prefers him, venerates, and esteems him; and that she defers to him, praises him, and loves and admires him exceedingly]."*

Ladies, if a man is not prepared to lavish on you his utmost love and devotion, then he is not worth your precious time. As a mature single woman, you need to be at the place where only the best is good enough for you, and nothing short of that. The thought that any man is better than no man is a cry of desperation, and this is not God's best for your life. Are you really prepared to forfeit your destiny for some smooth-talking snake in the grass? Don't be fooled by these men whom Satan will use to trap and deceive you and rob you of your destiny. If he has no respect for you now while you're dating, then believe me, it won't get any better once you're married to him. Trust me. And trust the testimony of countless women who thought they could change such a man, but failed. When these guys come across your path, because come they will, your guard should always be up. The alarm bells should be able to deafen you and jerk you out of the lull you may find yourself falling into. You should be asking yourself, "Will this man treat me the way God treats me?" "Will he carefully protect and cherish me the way he takes care of himself?" Your conscience will always be your best "girlfriend," so allow "her" to speak to you. The enemy's sole purpose is to defeat and trap you. The fact that you choose to keep your body pure in obedience to your true love (God) really bugs him. And if he has been successful in causing you to fall in this area, don't beat yourself up about it, as our Father is a forgiving God. When you repent and return to Him, He remembers your sin no more, and it becomes as if you had never sinned in that area. He restores your virginity as you now live in obedience and purity for Him. *(Read the latter part of Jeremiah 31:34: –"For I will forgive their iniquity, and I will [seriously] remember their sin no more" - TAB.* Also read *Hebrews 8:8-12,* and *10:16-17,* which supports this truth.)

Remember how *Isaiah 54:5* says that whilst you are living your single life, God is being a husband to you? Well, He will continue to carry on being your husband alongside that "natural" husband when he comes along. Therefore, do not rush into anything. Allow God — your "spiritual' husband" — to guide and protect your judgements. *"He leads the humble in what is right, and the humble He teaches His way" (Psalm 25:9 TAB). "I, [the Lord] will instruct you and teach you in the way you should go; I will counsel you with My eye upon you. Be not like the horse or the mule, which lack understanding, which must have their mouths held firm with bit and bridle, or else they will come with you. Many are the sorrows of the wicked, but he who trusts in, relies on, and confidently leans on the Lord shall be compassed about with mercy and with lovingkindness" (Psalm 32:8-10 TAB).*

When the time is right, God (your "spiritual" husband) will lead you to the right person, and with no insecurity or jealously on His part. He knows just the man that He has for you, and He will gladly and proudly release you into that person's care. Our part is to totally trust and confidently rely on Him, regardless of how long we have to wait. Because God is the one and only true love of your life, He is going to see to it that you receive the best; therefore, that should eliminate all anxiety and worry from your mind. It is also reassuring to know that you do not have to go on a wild goose chase looking for him (and if you do, you might end up with someone you did not quite bargain for). The Bible is full of stories of people who did not wait on God, and they unhappily reaped what they sowed. A classic example is the story of Abraham and Sarah *(Genesis 16 & 18),* who were promised a son and took matters into their own hands, all because they could not wait on God – and the Arabs and Jews are still at war to this very day because of the jealousy and enmity between Ishmael and Isaac from the very beginning, so don't be too hasty.

Another area we need to look at is the depth of our love for God. We often go to lengths to express our love for God, but in reality, how much do we truly love Him? Are the words "I love you God" just a cliché that rolls casually off our tongues, or do we have a personal and intimate relationship with God that reveals the extent of our love towards Him? A good indication when assessing our love for Him is found in the Word of God. In conversation with His disciples, Jesus challenged their thinking with a bold statement. *"If you [really] love me, you will keep (obey) my commandments" (John 14:15).*

Can it be that simple in proving to God that we really love Him, by living a life of righteousness based on His Holy Word? Whilst it could seem that some grand and elaborate scheme might be more appropriate for us to prove or show God the extent of our love, in actuality, all God asks of us is the basics –just be obedient to His commandments. God wants our love to be based on who He is to us, rather than focusing on what we can get from Him. Jesus went on to share with His disciples, *"The person who has My commands and keeps them is the one who [really] loves me; and whoever [really] loves me will be loved by my father and I (too) will love him and will show (reveal, manifest) Myself to him. [I will let Myself be clearly seen by him and make Myself real to him]" (John 14:21 TAB).*

God knows that when we earnestly and passionately pursue Him with a pure heart, without hidden agendas, we will be drawn into a place where He can begin to reveal and manifest to us the extent of who He really is. It is at this place where we find that we cannot help but abide under the shadow of the almighty (Psalm 91). Ladies, experiencing difficulties at this stage in our "love walk" with God, where we cannot appreciate that deep and intimate relationship with Him will filter through to our natural relationship when we eventually find our soul mate. Our intimate relationship with God will prepare us for that intimate relationship with our mate. If you are still at that stage in your life where you are waiting for Mr. Right, then perhaps whilst you are waiting you will turn the spotlight on the inside and examine your own relationship with God. What would be your response to the following questions?

- How desperate do you get for God?
- Is He the first thing on your mind when you awake and the last thing on your mind when you crawl into bed?
- When thinking of Him, do you sometimes find yourself smiling as you recall one of His kind gestures that He has done for you?
- Is there any person in your life that has your undivided attention more than God?
- When you hear His name, does it make you go weak at the knees and send a shiver down your spine?

How did you fare? Were you able to answer positively, or do you have a bit more work to do in developing your intimacy with Him? The reason I wanted to challenge your thinking in these areas is because we often have such feelings for a natural person. Have you thought about what will happen when you do eventually meet that guy? Will he get all the attention that you should be attributing to God? In examining our "love walk," it must be said that if we can channel these emotions to someone of the opposite sex, then surely we should be in a position to place our highest affections to the One whom we say is our one and only true love.

Therefore, putting everything that has been said in this chapter into perspective, I put the question to you again. When you say, "I love God," do you really love Him? And if your answer is still yes, then are you prepared to follow the route that will lead you to experience the ultimate ecstasy in God – His *agape* love?

Jesus wanted to ensure that His disciples grasped the truth of the matter in this chapter *(John 14)* and continued to share with them even more to the extent that they would be fully persuaded within their hearts. He wanted them to appreciate their relationship with Him so that they would transfer it from merely being head knowledge to a deep and lasting heartfelt experience in God. Jesus assured them by saying that *"If a person [really] loves me, He will keep My word [obey my teaching]; and My Father will love him, and we will come to him and make our home (abode, special dwelling place) with him"* (verse 23).

Ladies, make it a daily ritual to evaluate your "love walk" with God. It is important that you get your priorities in order. That means seeking Him first, and then everything else will fall into place. When we have evaluated our lives and have put God in His rightful place, then and only then will we be able to say this verse with confidence and conviction: *"For the [true] love of God is this: that we do His commands [keep His ordinances and are mindful of His precepts and teaching]. And these orders of His are not irksome [burdensome, oppressive or grievous]"* (1 John 5:3 TAB). When you really love God, His commandments will not seem hard or laborious, but the extent of your love will propel you to want to do anything that will please Him. This too is great preparation for pleasing that man whom God will send your way. So let God do for you what He so longs to do. There's a reason why He preserved you to be a mature single woman for such a time as this. Don't spoil it now. Don't settle for — dare I say it — corned beef, when you can have steak! (You know what I mean!) Wait for God's best, a man who will truly love you for who you are. And whilst you wait for God's best, take a little time out to spoil and pamper yourself. After all, you're worth it.

CHAPTER SEVEN

PAMPER YOURSELF – WHO ELSE WILL?

"Do you not know that your body is the temple (the very sanctuary) of the Holy Spirit Who lives within you, Whom you have received [as a Gift] from God? You are not your own, You were bought with a price [purchased with a preciousness and paid for, made His own]. So then, honour God and bring glory to Him in your body"
(1 Corinthians 6:19-20 TAB)

Now ladies, you should really enjoy reading this chapter, because you get the opportunity to be selfish for a change and concentrate on you, all done perfectly above-board and in a way that is acceptable and pleasing to God.

As a mature single woman, it is okay to want to look good and treat yourself to nice things when you can. After all, you do not have a husband to share the money with. And if you do not have any children either, you have got to spend the money on someone – so why not spend it on you? And there should be no reason to feel guilty either; after all, this is just one of the perks of being single.

For us women, feeling good about ourselves is usually associated with the way we look. However, we first need to be happy within and learn to love ourselves, which will make us want to look after the outer woman also. I used to associate feeling good about myself with the way my hair looked. It didn't matter what my clothes looked like, or how I felt inside, as long as my hair was neat and suitably styled, I felt good. However, when I started to have problems with my hair, I found that I could not allow my feelings to be dictated just because of the way my hair looked. I had to learn to wake up every day feeling good about myself, even if my hair did not look its best.

In the day and age that we are living in, there are so many ways that a woman can pamper herself. Number one, and most importantly, we should look after our bodies. That means learning to maintain a healthy lifestyle, which includes taking responsibility for what we eat and ensuring that our bodies get regular exercise. Concentrating on these two areas alone will help us feel energetic and lively and give us stamina to lead an active and healthy life.

We also feel a lot better about ourselves when we are close to the average weight for our height, which gives us energy and often boosts our confidence levels. Ladies, here's a "heavy revvy" for you (meaning heavy revelation): men are visual beings who are usually attracted to women based on what they see. Therefore, if what they are seeing does not attract them, they will usually move on until they find what they're envisioning in their mind's eye as the perfect woman for them. So if you feel your body needs toning up or you need to lose a few pounds, perhaps you might think about joining a gym. This is another way of getting out and meeting new people, so you are "killing two birds with one stone." You develop friendships and get a great shape at the same time. What could be better? (Then again, you may be happy with the way you are, and this too is fine. You should always feel good about yourself and not have to conform to what others think you should look like). So don't beat up on yourself; I am not purporting that you should look like some of those skinny sticks you see on the magazine covers, but what I am promoting is that you adopt a healthier lifestyle, which is more beneficial health-wise in the long run.

Let's take a look at Esther, a single woman in the Bible who underwent an extensive beauty treatment programme when she was in competition with hundreds of other ladies vying for the King's attention to be the next queen. King Ahasuerus was looking for a new queen, and Esther was amongst those chosen to prepare themselves for him. Because of Esther's beauty, she was noticed instantly by his attendants *(Esther 2:7)*. She was given maids to assist her and the best apartment in the king's harem *(Esther 2:9)*. Can you imagine? — it took twelve months of preparation before she could even see the king. It is obvious that a great deal of importance was placed on their physical appearance and that the women eat the right kinds of food. *"Now when the turn of each maiden came to go in to King Ahasuerus, after the regulations for the women had been carried out for twelve months – since this was the regular period for their beauty treatments, six months with oil and myrrh and six months with sweet spices and perfumes and the things for the purifying of the women. Then in this way the maiden came to the king; whatever she desired was given her to take with her from the harem into the king's palace" (Esther 2:12-13 TAB)*.

This beauty treatment with oils, myrrh, sweet spices, and perfumes sounds a bit like the equivalent to our aromatherapy spa treatments. Nevertheless, it worked. It did the trick, and Esther got her man (Ladies, see what a bit of lipstick and a splash of perfume will do for you!). *"And the king loved Esther more than all the women, and she obtained grace and favour in his sight more than all the maidens, so that he set the royal crown on her head and made her queen instead of Vashti" (Esther 2:17)*. Had Esther not taken the time to pamper herself in such an extravagant way, perhaps the king would not have noticed her. However, God had a plan for Esther's life which would involve saving her entire nation, and if this vigorous beauty routine was what was needed to get Esther in a strategic place to be noticed, then so be it. It makes you wonder, though, what God has up His sleeve for you and me, wouldn't you agree?

You may not have the patience of Esther – you may feel that twelve months is a long time to work on your body; however, you should take the time to treat yourself occasionally to something you have never done before. How about a sauna — have you ever tried one? I have been to the sauna a couple of times, and it has been a relaxing way to unwind whilst also allowing the pores in my body to be cleansed and refreshed. Speaking of saunas let me share a humorous story with you. Whilst on holiday one year, I got the shock of my life when I went to the sauna at Center Parcs with my sister and cousin. We did not realise it was a mixed session, and as we entered the booth, to our horror we saw this scrawny little man sprawled on the back bench revealing his entire nudity. We spent the entire time giggling like a bunch of schoolgirls – it really was funny. So if you are new to the 'sauna scene,' perhaps you might want to check beforehand whether it is a mixed session or a females-only session, if only to save yourself any unnecessary embarrassment and horrible 'flashbacks' (yuk)!

Health farms and spas are also becoming quite popular these days. Why not treat yourself to a couple of days off from work, and perhaps you and a friend could book yourself into one. Let yourself be spoiled to the max, from head to toe. Even though I have yet to visit one, I can imagine that women leave there feeling totally relaxed and tranquil, ready to face the mayhem of the real world again.

Be sure to treat yourself to facials every now and again. The experts tell us that it is very important that we look after our skin and protect it for later on in life. You could also treat yourself by having your nails done by a professional manicurist. This too has proved very popular of late. Many ladies in the church where I attend have their nails manicured regularly, and it adds such an elegant touch. It is also another way of feeling good about your womanhood. I am sure you get the picture by now that it is nice to look good and feel attractive. And I believe that if God has allowed us to have access to such luxuries, then it would be crazy not to make use of them (and let's be honest ladies, some of us do need a bit of help – smile!)

Spending time with friends is also something that we singles love to do. I love to go to the cinema and watch a good movie, especially if it is romantic. I am not into horror or films of an evil nature, and I also like a film that will humour me. It is nice to get out regularly and not coop yourself up at home being bored and feeling lonely. Have you ever thought about going to the theatre? The atmosphere is a lot different from that of a cinema. It is more interactive, and it also makes you feel special that you have taken the time to entertain yourself in a classy way that is a bit above the norm. Over the years I have been to see many performances, all of which have been thoroughly enjoyable. So ladies, when you begin to see your worth and realise that you are allowed to enjoy the finer things of life, you will start doing a lot more with your life and not waste it moping around, losing valuable time.

And finally, I know you are probably wondering when I was going to get to the "shop till you drop" part. Well, tighten your seat belts, because we're here now. Yes, ladies, treat yourselves to new outfits, new shoes, bags, jewellery, and perfumes, etc., all within reason, of course. If you have to go into debt to treat yourself to such delights, then it defeats the purpose and it is definitely not worth it (been there, done that, got the T-shirt), as well, this goes against God's Word concerning being a good steward of the money He has blessed you with. But if you have allowed God's wisdom to help you in your finances, and you have reached that place where you spend only what you have (and you give to the Lord's work according to the commandments in His Word), then it's quite acceptable for you to treat yourself to nice things.

If God has found you to be a faithful steward over His finances, then it just might be that He has blessed you expressly so that you can be a blessing to others. Be kind to your family and friends and bless them also. Treat them to nice things also, with no hidden agendas, wanting nothing back in return. *"Give, and [gifts] will be given to you; good measure, pressed down, shaken together, and running over, will they pour into [the pouch formed by] the bosom [of your robe and used as a bag]. For with the measure you deal out [with the measure you use when you confer benefits on others], it will be measured back to you"* (Luke 6:38 TAB).

Singles are often wrongly accused of being selfish, only thinking about "Number One." But as a woman who has been single for a number of years, I would argue that this is not necessarily the case. Our self-confidence is sometimes perceived as arrogance or self-centredness, mainly because the lives of others are more of a struggle financially and otherwise. The truth is that we have made a decision to enjoy our lives and live it to the fullest (See Chapter 4, Live Your Life "in the Now"). We have learnt that we only get one shot at this life on planet Earth, and so we refuse to let one moment pass us by meaningless. And yes, it may mean that as mature single women we can have the best money can buy, but this comes about solely because of our single status in life and how God has blessed our lives. God is the one who has ordained that we should be single, for how many years He sees fit, and therefore we can only do what we know how to do, and that is to **live.** *Psalm 37:23* depicts this beautifully (I've personalised it for us ladies): *"The steps of a [good] woman are directed and established by the Lord when He delights in her way [and He busies Himself with her every step]" (TAB).*

So ladies, don't feel guilty because of the fact that you can pamper yourself, treat yourself to extravagant clothes, have a classy car, or travel to great places. God has given you this freedom, and *"whom the son has set free, is free indeed" (John 8:36).* When you live an exemplary life for God and walk blameless before Him, there should be no feelings of condemnation, for God rewards faithfulness.

Satan is the instigator of these guilty feelings. *John 10:10* says that his whole purpose in life is to steal from you, which includes your joy, your peace of mind, and anything else he can take from you. *"The thief comes only in order to steal and kill and destroy. I came that they might have and enjoy life, and have it in abundance (to the full, till it overflows)" (TAB).* Therefore, ladies, whose report are you going to believe — God's report of life or Satan's report of death? If Satan could, he would suck the very life out of us, but God gave His son, Jesus, who brought us life. In *Romans 8:1-2* we are reminded that *"there is therefore now no condemnation to them which are in Christ Jesus, who walk not after the flesh, but after the Spirit. For the law of the Spirit of life in Christ Jesus hath made me free from the law of sin and death" (KJV).*

You have been given your single lifestyle as a gift for a God-given purpose, so take the time to enjoy it. Please do not misunderstand what I am saying. I am not advocating that married women cannot pamper themselves also and go on wild spending sprees too (because some of them are in a position to do so). However, what I am saying is that the singles are not accountable to any one person and do not need permission from a spouse, and therefore have more liberty than the married in this area. I am sure that one day, however, when we eventually marry, we too will be tamed in this area, but until then, shop till you drop, girlfriends, and enjoy it.

Chapter Eight

BUT GOD, MY BIOLOGICAL CLOCK IS TICKING ... LOUDLY!

*" ... Let God be found true though every
human being is false and a liar, as it is written,
That You may be justified and shown to be
upright in what You say, and prevail when
You are judged [by sinful men]"
(Romans 3:4 TAB).*

As a mature single, you may be established in your singleness in terms of having a good career and being financially secure. You may be able to afford going on exotic holidays, and may own property, a car, and the like. Within your heart of hearts, though, you hope and expect to get married some day. However, there is an element that is often not discussed amongst mature singles, and that is the desire to know the joys of motherhood and be fulfilled in that area of their lives, if this is not a role they already fulfil. The commonly-used saying for this strong desire is that a woman's "biological clock is ticking."

There is much truth in this statement, but as Christian women we are to be patient and wait on the Lord regarding this area. *"Wait on the Lord: be of good courage, and He shall strengthen thine heart: wait I say, on the Lord"* (Psalms 27:14 KJV). In other words, God is saying that our desires are natural and legitimate, but that we should wait on Him to bring them to pass, and that if we try to make those desires happen on our own, we will get out of His will for our lives. *Job 6:8* states, *"Oh that I might have my request, and that God would grant me the thing that I long for"* (TAB). A lot of the time we allow the world to pressure and dictate to us what we should have achieved by a certain age, when in reality we should be looking to God and the Bible to shed light on the standards He requires us to live by. The news media scares us with statistics about the increased risks involved in having children over the age of 40, but let us take heart in the truth of this scripture: *"Let God be true and every man a liar"* (Romans 3:4). We can either allow ourselves to be sucked in by the world's fears of how things should be, or we can put our future and trust wholeheartedly in the almighty God who is in total control of everything.

The stories of two particularly elderly women in the Bible who became mothers at a late age are recorded to give mature single women great hope and encouragement in the area of childbearing. Namely, Elisabeth and Sarah, and who were also, I might add, both a lot older than 30/40. So if motherhood is a desire of yours, then don't give up hope. In fact, the Bible says Elisabeth was *"well stricken in years" (Luke 1:18 KJV)*. And Sarah was so shocked at the news of her pregnancy that she said, *"who would have said unto Abraham, that Sarah should have given children suck? For I have born him a son <u>in his old age</u>" (Genesis 21:7 KJV)*. Ladies, let's not get anxious about the future when we haven't even gotten there yet. *("Therefore I tell you, do not worry about your life, what you will eat or drink; or about your body, what you will wear" (Matthew 6:25 NIV)*. Just know that God is faithful, and He will give us the desires of our hearts, if children are what we desire. *"Delight yourself in the Lord and he will give you the desires of your heart" (Psalms 37:4 NIV)*. His plans for us are for good and not for evil. His plans are to give us peace and an expected end *(Jeremiah 29:11)*. God had a plan for these two godly women. He understood their heartfelt cry and their need to have a child, and He did not let their age dictate to Him what He knew His power could override. When God makes us a promise, He will bring it to pass, but in His own time. In *Romans 4 (TAB)*, Abraham and Sarah's story is beautifully portrayed. *Verses 19-21: "He did not weaken in faith when he considered the [utter] impotence of his body, which was <u>as good as dead</u> because he was about hundred years old, or [when he considered] the barrenness of Sarah's [deadened] womb. (See also Genesis 17:17; 18:11.)*

No unbelief or distrust made him waver (doubtingly question) concerning the promise of God, but he grew strong and was empowered by faith as he gave praise and glory to God, fully satisfied and assured that God was able and mighty to keep His word and to do what He had promised" (TAB). What great faith in God. *Verse 20* in the King James Version states that Abraham *"staggered not at the promise of God through unbelief; but was strong in faith, giving glory to God."*

No wonder God called him the Father of Faith. This is the kind of faith we are to have, a faith that does not "stagger at God's promises through unbelief." Even though the years may creep up on us and some people will make their own assumptions, we are to be strong in the Lord and give Him the glory at every season of our lives.

Sarah defeated the odds. What are the odds, you may ask. The odds are those limitations that others put on us when they cannot "see" anything happening in our lives. But we are to have absolute, unwavering faith in God, without which it is impossible to please Him. *"And without faith it is impossible to please God, because anyone who comes to him must believe that he exists and that he rewards those who earnestly seek him" (Hebrews 11:6).* We are to have faith that is tenacious and unmoved by what it sees or feels, a faith that is unshakeable in God. If God's Word has given you a promise, then that faith rises up and says, "I'm going to wait on God, regardless of the circumstances; God will come through for me." Therefore, take courage and trust God's Word, which declares that you will not suffer barrenness, miscarriages or be unfruitful. These promises are found in the following scriptures: *Exodus 23:26; Deuteronomy 7:14; Psalm 113:9; Isaiah 54:1; Malachi 3:11; Luke 23:29; Galatians 4:27; and 2 Peter 1:8.*

Sadly, not everyone puts their trust in God, waiting for His perfect timing in their lives, and may look to alternative routes to have a child. One such route is being artificially inseminated with donor sperm using a sperm bank. This is a route that seems to be on the increase and is being adopted by a number of Hollywood singles who perceive this as the new way of conceiving and becoming a mother without a father figure on the scene. However, as godly single women, we cannot adopt worldly principles to fulfil our heartfelt desires. We should not even consider this alternative, because it has all kinds of ethical and moral issues associated with it.

When we choose the option of artificial insemination, we take our future out of God's hands and put it into the hands of man. Let's take a closer look at the idea of artificial insemination. When looking up the word 'artificial' in the Reader's Digest Universal Dictionary[1] it gives the definition as 1. "**Made by man** rather than occurring in nature." 2. "Made **in imitation of something natural**." 3. "**Feigned, pretended**." The definition it gives for the actual concept of artificial insemination is, "The introduction of semen into the female reproductive organs **by means other than sexual contact**."

I believe these definitions make it very plain that it is an unnatural process, which **excludes** the

Omnipotence of God from the process. From the beginning it has been God's design for a husband and wife to reproduce and replenish the earth. *Genesis 1:27-28 (KJV)* reveals, *"So God created man in His own image, in the image of God created He him; male and female created He them. And God blessed them, and God said unto them, be fruitful, and multiply, and replenish the earth, and subdue it, and have dominion over the fish of the sea, and over the fowl of the air, and over every living thing that moveth upon the earth." (See also Genesis 4:1 (NKJV): Now Adam knew Eve **his wife**, and she conceived and bore Cain, and said, 'I have acquired a man from the LORD.' Then she bore again, this time his brother Abel.")*

From the beginning of time Satan has used deception to cause us to doubt the Word of God. He always has an alternative plan to what God's Word has promised, which we know as his 'counterfeits.' For a single woman to have a child through artificial insemination is just another counterfeit plan of his to get mankind to disregard God's standards for marriage. By taking something that is supposed to be a natural process between a husband and a wife, his plan is to use this as a tool for his own gain. Please don't misunderstand; I am not saying that children who are born by this method are not unique and precious, because in God's sight, all life is precious. What I am implying, however, is that Satan's number one priority in life is to get people to do things in their own strength, pushing God aside as they achieve their own selfish desires.

A similar occurrence happened at the beginning of time when a group of people got together to build a tower to reach God. This is what they purposed in their hearts: *"And they said, go to, let us build us a city and a tower, whose top may reach unto heaven; and let us make us a name, lest we be scattered abroad upon the face of the whole earth" (Genesis 11:4 KJV).* And note God's response to their unity: *"And the Lord said, behold, they are one people and they have all one language; and this is only the beginning of what they will do, **and now nothing they have imagined they can do will be impossible to them.** Come, let us go down and there confound (mix up, confuse) their language, that they may not understand one another's speech" (verse 6-7 TAB).* Satan will take a tool God designed for good to bring about his evil plans. God has given scientists the knowledge and breakthroughs in research to find cures for innumerable diseases. However, Satan then causes some of those same scientists to go another step forward into implementing procedures that exclude God and go against His very nature and design.

Finally, and probably what I find most alarming regarding the whole issue on artificial insemination, is the idea of a single woman having sperm injected into her body that was originally from a man whom she knows nothing about. And if the Bible speaks against singles engaging in premarital sex, then surely this too would be wrong, because it is the same principle, only without the physical contact and intercourse taking place.

Therefore, as we delve deeper into this subject, we can clearly see that this is not a path God has chosen for us mature singles to take, even if our biological clock is ticking ... loudly! And even if you were successful in having a healthy child through this method, what could you tell him/her about their father when at an appropriate age they started getting curious as to who he was, what he looked like, and what was his name, as well as other important questions? And to make matters worse, when it comes time for your son or daughter to get married, what guarantees would you have that the person they are marrying is not actually their half sister or brother or a first cousin? I know the latter sounds far-fetched, but it could happen, especially in small communities.

I know the above paragraphs contain a lot of controversial information to digest, but these issues have serious implications, and some mature singles who are desperate for a child might consider such options without looking at the real risks, which is clearly outside the will of God for their lives. However, to alleviate any of your anxieties and fears, please be assured that God is in control of everything. And at the right time, when you have settled down with the one that you want to have children with, He will not hold back from giving you the desires of your heart.

So in your time of waiting in this particular season of your life, learn to have a song in your heart. This song could be based on your dreams and what you are believing God will do in your life. One such song is taken from *Isaiah 54: 1: "Sing, O barren, thou that didst not bear; break forth into singing, and cry aloud, thou that didst not travail with child: for more are the children of the desolate than the children of the married wife, saith the Lord" (KJV).* Your job now is to keep that ticking clock under control and not to let its noise overwhelm you. *"And let us not lose heart and grow weary and faint in acting nobly and doing right, for in* **due time and at the appointed season we shall reap**, *if we do not loosen and relax our courage and faint" (Galatians 6:9 TAB).*

I realise that the older we get, we will tend to focus on the physical aspect that perhaps we will not be able to bear children. However, we really have to let go of the worry in this area and give it to God and watch Him unfold His awesome plan predestined for us. Another promise in His Word that we can stand on regarding this area is taken from *Isaiah 66:9: "Shall I bring to the [moment of] birth and not cause to bring forth? Says the Lord. Shall I who causes to bring forth shut the womb? Says your God" (TAB).* In other words, God is directing our anxieties towards Him as the Omnipotent God. This verse assures us that when we eventually find our soul mate, we are not going to be faced with the disappointment of thinking that we are too old and cannot bear children (if we are medically able to). God says He will not allow our wombs to be shut, and that He will cause us to bring forth. That should extinguish all such fears that the enemy uses to taunt us with. God is the source of life. Our priority must be to look to God as the source of life and trust His Word, not looking at our circumstances or allowing society to rewrite our predestined future.

Chapter Nine

TO BE OR NOT TO BE – THAT IS THE QUESTION

"Actually, I don't have a sense of needing anything personally. I've learned by now to be quite content whatever my circumstances. I'm just as happy with little as with much, with much as with little. I've found the recipe for being happy whether full or hungry, hands full or hands empty. Whatever I have, wherever I am, I can make it through anything in the One who makes me who I am"
(Philippians 4:11-13 TM).

The previous chapter talked about those women whose biological clocks seem to be "tick, tick, tocking away." However, in contrast to such women, I've spoken to numerous mature singles that have come to terms with the fact that they probably will never become a mother, even after they are married, for whatever reason, and therefore I felt that this controversial issue was too important to exclude from a book for mature singles. And this reasoning has not come about just because they feel that they are too old to become a mother, for we know that nothing is impossible with our God. We only have to look at His track record of successfully blessing older women with children to dismiss such a notion (as mentioned in the previous chapter using Sarah and Elisabeth as examples). However, there may be other underlying factors, such as medical reasons, why some mature singles may have personally come to this decision for their individual lives.

"To be or not to be; that is the question" is a famous quote from one of William Shakespeare's more popular plays namely Hamlet[1]. In this story, the hero finds himself struggling with two opposing forces. And mature singles will be only too familiar struggling with a similar scenario. To be or not to be a mother, once they are married, that is the question. And if you desire not to be a mother, for whatever personal reasons you conclude, then there is always the guilt in justifying it to yourself and others as to why this is so.

As stated above, there are other underlying factors that may bring mature singles to come to such a decision. Personally, I know for me, the years of living as a single woman for such a long time can bring a person to come to such a decision, however, I am not ruling motherhood out just yet, this is just something that hasn't happened yet. I sincerely believe that when

Insightful Tips for the Unique "Mature" Single

I meet someone with whom I intend to share the rest of my life with, then I may feel differently, if that is a road we choose together to take, but having children has not been a priority in my life. To be honest, I have never really been the motherly type and was always made fun of by family members when they saw my attempts at changing a baby's nappy. I was once timed and videoed by my cousin as I changed her baby at his christening (he's now 11). Everyone found it hilarious, only because it was something I never did and the whole concept was quite foreign to me, and not to mention the sweat that was pouring off my forehead at the time.

Even now, my brother has two girls and my younger sister often offers to have them over and does all the playful 'auntie things' with them. However, this is not something that I instinctively do. Don't get me wrong, I do love children and am grateful for the opportunity to input into their lives; I'm just not a natural. But I do get involved and I currently work at my local church in the children's ministry which, whilst challenging, I find extremely rewarding.

Whilst I would have preferred to had been married and had children in my younger days, as I said earlier, I have not closed the door in this area. As mature singles we cannot always envision what blessings God has in store for those who are faithful to His Word, and therefore we should always live in an atmosphere of expectancy. *"No eye has seen, no ear has heard, no mind has conceived what God has prepared for those who love Him" (1 Corinthians 2: 9 NIV).* At this particular time in my life I feel quite content to be single, but this is only because I have had years of practice and have learnt to develop in this way. Paul stated that he learnt to be content no matter what the circumstances *(Philippians 4:11)*.

I have friends of a similar age who I have asked how they feel with regard to this subject and the reactions have been mixed. I believe that as mature singles we can get to a stage in our lives and conclude that because we are not married yet, then motherhood is not for us. But if motherhood is something you really desire, then don't allow the fact that you are single to deter you from waiting on God for your heartfelt desires, but continue to dream and hope and exercise your faith in the realms of whatever contradictions the enemy may present. However, if you feel that you are content with where your life is and that this is a road which you feel you do not wish to embark on, then don't feel condemned either. Just continue to follow the leading of God for your individual life and do not worry about what others may think.

It may be that you feel you could best serve God as a single and therefore would prefer to remain unmarried. Anna was a prophetess in the Bible who decided not to remarry after she became a widow; she devoted herself wholeheartedly to the work of the Lord *(Luke 2:36-37)*. Paul also gives his slant on individuals remaining single which, whilst he seems to be speaking to men, can be interpreted generically here. *"On the other hand, if a man is comfortable in his decision for a single life in service to God and it's entirely his own conviction and not imposed on him by others, he ought to stick with it" (1 Corinthians 3:37 TM).*

So even though this book has been offering insightful tips to mature single women in their wait for Mr. Right, you may have already chosen to wholeheartedly devote yourself in service to God as an unmarried single. And whilst such a decision may automatically put you in the category of not fulfilling a maternal role, God still blesses individuals with opportunities to be aunts and god-parents to children. And it's through avenues like these that we are able to show affection in ways that may not have been possible because we were not able to physically fulfil a maternal role.

So, unique mature single, where do we go from here? There really is no other option and therefore the answer is simple. We have to look to God who is in complete control of our lives, and we have to be honest with Him regarding our feelings about this delicate area of our lives. If marriage-and-motherhood is something you desire and see in your future, then hold on to that desire and do not let it go, regardless of how bleak things might look. If on the other hand you have already fought that battle in your mind and have decided that you do not need to be a mother to be fulfilled as a person, then also hold on to that desire. We shouldn't feel condemned about any decision we make for our lives, as it is between us and God and no other third party apart, of course, from the person we eventually marry. Woman of God be encouraged by the scripture which states *"For God has not given us a spirit of fear and timidity, but of power, love and self-discipline" (2 Timothy 1: 7 NLT).*

Chapter Ten

SQUARE PEGS DON'T FIT INTO ROUND HOLES

"Do not be unequally yoked with unbelievers [do not make mismated alliances with them or come under a different yoke with them, inconsistent with your faith]. For what partnership have right living and right standing with God with iniquity and lawlessness? Or how can light have fellowship with darkness?"
(2 Corinthians 6:14 TAB)

This is a subject that a number of women have had difficulty with at some stage or another in their lives. It is especially common with women who have reached a point where they reason with themselves that they would like to get married any time soon. With the ratio of twice more single women than men being a reality in Christian circles, the women will always feel that there are not enough men in the church to go around. However this factor should not be an excuse for us to take matters into our own hands when looking for a suitable mate.

I'm sure most of us have sat in conferences, heard tapes, and listened to speakers on numerous occasions talk about the risks involved in being unequally yoked together in marriage with an unbeliever. However, we may still go on to believe that this route is our only option left, because of what we think we are seeing with our physical eyes, whilst failing to "see" with our spiritual eyes. The Bible is very clear on this subject, and as mature Christian women we are not to take this matter lightly, but are to heed the signposts that the Holy Spirit will give to us in regard to this area.

The story of Samson in the book of *Judges, chapters 13-16,* paints the perfect picture of what happens when you choose a mate who is outside of your faith. Samson was chosen by God and set apart to be a Nazirite unto God from the womb. Therefore, we can see that from Samson's inception, God had a specific purpose for his life. God has a specific purpose for each and every one of our lives, and whilst Satan does not know the exact details of that purpose, he sets out with his own agenda to frustrate the plan of God.

As a mature single, God has already purposed in His heart to give you the best – a man of God – there is no doubt about this. No matter what you can or cannot see happening, the plan has already been constructed from the foundations of the world.

"Even as [in His love] He chose us [actually picked us out for Himself as His own] in Christ before the foundation of the world, that we should be holy (consecrated and set apart for Him) and blameless in His sight, even above reproach, before Him in love" (Ephesians 1:4 TAB).

Samson had a code of conduct which he was required to live by according to *Judges 13:7*. Similarly, we too have a code of conduct as set forth in the Word of God. When we fail to comply with the requirements of that code of conduct, we fall prey to disastrous paths that God did not purpose for us to experience in His original, perfect plan for our lives.

Samson went for the "forbidden fruit" when he chose to go down to the Philistine camp at Timnah and there saw a woman that he immediately wanted for his wife *(see Judges 14:1-2)*. Samson's main reason for wanting this Philistine woman (a woman whose culture was in total opposition to his faith) was because she was pleasing to him *(v. 3)*. In other words, on the surface, she looked right in his eyes. However, Samson's attraction was based purely on externals, and he overlooked the most important part that we should all look for in a mate – a person's character and inner being, which will always reveal who or what that person is really like.

We have already ascertained that Samson was set apart specifically to be used by God, and, according to *Numbers 6:1-8*, a Nazirite was to live every day for God and not separate himself from God in any way. In other words, any decisions Samson made should have been consistent with his faith, and more importantly, he should have sought God's approval on a subject as important as choosing a wife. Singles, we are called to be Christians and like the Nazirites, we also are to live our lives holy each day. *"So, come out from among [unbelievers], and separate (sever) yourselves from them, says the Lord, and touch not [any] unclean thing; then I will receive you kindly and treat you with favour" (2 Corinthians 6:17 TAB).*

Samson begins his descent down the "slippery slope" to destruction first by not heeding his parents' warning about marrying a woman in total opposition to his faith and beliefs *(v.3)*, and then by choosing a wife from his rivals, the Philistines. From *verse 7* we see that Samson gets to know the woman and is well pleased with her, and so they get married. Sadly, because of his disobedience — ignoring the signposts God placed along the way — this marriage was doomed from the start. What started out to be instant attraction (what some people might call love at first sight) ended in Samson finding out what her true character was like as early as during the wedding feast celebrations. Her love of her people and culture was stronger than her love for Samson, and this ignored factor was the cause of their marriage breaking down and Samson's wife being given to his best friend by her father *(Judges 14:10-20)*. His wife should have left her people and cleaved to her husband *(Genesis 2:24)*, but she had no intentions of being a submissive wife.

So let's take a closer look at some of the factors that indicated the imminent failure of this marriage, even before it had a chance to flourish.

Insightful Tips for the Unique "Mature" Single

(1) Samson and his wife were not "equally yoked." Spiritually they were pulling in different directions. Quite understandably, in any unequally yoked situation the continual pulling in different directions will cause an impact and eventually a **snap** and a **separation** will occur.

(2) Samson did not seek God's direction in this area of his life, but instead allowed his fleshly desires to dictate to him.

(3) Samson ignored the warning signs that no doubt were visible along the way, the main one being his parents' advice.

(4) Samson bypassed what he knew was right for a person of his convictions (as a Nazirite) to pursue that which was forbidden.

Ladies, the forbidden area of your life that you will not give up and surrender to God will be the cause of your downfall and will utterly destroy you *(Judges 16:5)*. And in Samson's case it was his love of "strange" women *(read Proverbs 5:1-6 TAB)*. The result was that his marriage did not last. One good thing about our mistakes, however, is that God always allows us to learn from them, and with maturity and hindsight, hopefully we will not make the same errors again. One would think Samson would have learnt his lesson concerning pursuing Philistine women, but his failure to learn from that marriage led to his weakness in being manipulated by Delilah, another Philistine woman who was used by Satan as a tool to frustrate Samson's destiny and bring about his eventual downfall.

Are you dealing with a forbidden relationship in your life? Is there a man/men who God has repeatedly told you to leave (or have nothing to do with) and for some reason or the other you cannot quite bring yourself to end that relationship? Think long and hard about what you are doing in allowing yourself to continue in this relationship. You may have convinced yourself that you are such a strong person spiritually that you will be able to win that person to God. However, nine times out of ten, the opposite happens and the unbeliever succeeds in drawing the Christian away from the things of God – which ultimately is Satan's plan in the first place.

There was no doubt that Samson was strong — everyone knew it, but Satan used Samson's weakness for ungodly women to destroy him. Samson's "love" (more likely it was lust) of these women caused him to disregard the little nudges that the Holy Spirit was giving to him.

Why is it that Samson could not discern what Delilah was up to? She constantly tried to coax from him the source of his strength. And even though he tricked her on a few occasions as to what his secret was, he still did not "put two and two together" when eventually the Philistines came upon him with the same plan he had previously entrusted to her. Could the phrase "love is blind" be a classic example here? I believe as Christian women, the Holy Spirit gives us discernment and wisdom in choosing our relationships. Therefore, we are to pay attention to any warning signs He shows us when He sees that we are diverting from the route He has designed for us. *Proverbs 1:7* tells us that *"The fear of the Lord is the beginning of knowledge: but <u>fools despise wisdom and instruction" (KJV)</u>.* Let's not be fools in the area of our relationships.

Let's look to God for guidance in all areas of our lives and especially in helping us choose a mate wisely. It is not God's will that we marry a man who is inconsistent with our faith, as highlighted in *Colossians 2:8: "See to it that no one carries you off as spoil or makes you yourselves captive by his so-called philosophy and intellectualism and vain deceit (idle fancies and plain nonsense), following human tradition (men's ideas of the material rather than the spiritual world), just crude notions following the rudimentary and elemental teachings of the universe and disregarding [the teachings of] Christ (the Messiah)" (TAB).*

Delilah continued to be persistent with her deception and hard work in wooing and sweet-talking Samson; she eventually pried his secret from him, and Samson's life changed instantly. In *Judges 16:20* it tells us that Samson got up as usual, shook and encouraged himself that he would be prepared to meet the Philistines, but this time it was different — he was not aware that "the presence of God had left him."

There is a danger that we too can go through the motions of thinking that God is with us, when in fact our sins have driven Him away from us. *Proverbs 10:9 shows us that "He who walks uprightly walks securely, but he who takes a crooked way shall be found out and punished" (TAB)*. Samson's bad choice of making an alliance with the wrong type of woman cost him his life. Similarly, if we make wrong choices in choosing a mate, it too will cost us our destiny. This story in Judges is just one of many highlighted in the Bible to bring to our awareness the impending dangers of being unequally yoked in marriage with an unbeliever.

Again, in *1 Kings 11:1-4 (TAB)* there is a similar account in the life of King Solomon, with the main difference being that he didn't have just one woman to contend with; in fact, Solomon had 700 wives and 300 concubines – he was quite 'the man.' *"They were of the very nations of whom the Lord said to the Israelites, <u>you shall not</u> mingle with them, <u>neither shall</u> they mingle with you, for surely <u>they will turn away your hearts</u> after their gods. Yet Solomon clung to these in love" (verse 2)*. These women, just like Delilah, turned Solomon's heart away from God, with the result being that his relationship with God was affected for the worst and not for the better *(verse 4)*. Ladies, be encouraged that the man God brings into your life is meant to enhance your life, not to bring it down to a level that is way below your worth and standard as a godly woman whose future is bright and prosperous – and if you wait for such a man, he will be worth it.

In bringing this subject to a close, as a visual lesson I would like to take you back to your childhood days. One of the first things we learnt as children was the ability to put blocks into holes that matched their shape. The square peg went into the square hole and the round peg into the round hole. However, whilst learning, we sometimes got frustrated because we tried, with some difficulty, to squeeze a square peg into a round hole. Do you remember how it would not fit? Can you remember what we had to do? We had to try every shape until the right shape fitted into the right hole, and in our understanding we learnt what shapes belonged together. Therefore, as you strive to be that woman of excellence, stop trying to force someone into your life that does not belong there – remember that what is yoked together unequally will eventually **break and cause a separation** – and divorce definitely is not God's best for His daughters. When it comes to choosing your soul mate, raise your expectations; hold out for the best, because you deserve a godly marriage that is designed by your Maker (the one with the blueprint for your life). Such a marriage will bring honour to God and the two of you as a couple, and it will be an example to others as they emulate and pattern their lives according to your blueprint.

Chapter Eleven

'NO RINGY, NO THINGY!' – RAISE YOUR EXPECTATIONS, BECAUSE YOU'RE WORTH SO MUCH MORE

"Now as to the matters of which you wrote me. It is well [and by that I mean advantageous, expedient, profitable, and wholesome] for a man not to touch a woman [to cohabit with her] but to remain unmarried. But because of the temptation to impurity and to avoid immorality, let each [man] have his own wife and let each [woman] have her own husband"
(1 Corinthians 7:1-2 TAB).

So let's get down to the nitty-gritty in this chapter; let's talk about sex. After all, everybody else talks about it. The advertisement industry uses sex to sell its products in a provocative and sensual way. From fast cars to chocolate bars, and even something as simple as toothpaste, the industry will in some way or another use sexual images and carnal connotations to promote their product. We are also bombarded daily by the entertainment industry with images of couples cohabiting, fornicating, and committing adultery. It has become the norm to believe that marriage is old fashioned, and Christians can easily get caught up in this way of thinking.

You will often hear comments such as, "I don't believe I need a piece of paper to prove that I love so and so." Many people think that the only difference between marriage and living together is just a legal piece of paper. Couples will therefore choose this lifestyle rather than choose God's way of committing to each other in holy matrimony. By deluding people into thinking this way, Satan accomplishes what he has done since the beginning of time – he deceives them. He uses deception to get us to take the principles of God and turn them into a lie or to belittle them as having no importance in today's modern society. *Genesis 3:1* confirms this: *"Now the serpent was more subtle and crafty than any living creature of the field which the Lord God had made. And he [Satan] said to the woman, can it really be that God has said you shall not eat from every tree of the garden?" - (TAB)*

Not only were Adam and Eve the first man and woman on planet Earth, but also they're the first that we read of in the Bible who were attracted to each other. However, God did not allow them to be joined together sexually until they became husband and wife – which is what I am referring to humorously when I say "no ringy, no thingy." *Genesis 2:24* states, *"Therefore a man shall leave his father and his mother and shall become united and cleave to his wife <u>and they shall</u> <u>become one flesh</u>" (TAB).*

When two people are joined together sexually, they become one in God's eyes whether they realise it or not. The two individuals have joined into a spiritual relationship and their souls have become tied to one another to a certain extent. Not only are their bodies joined together physically, but they are also joined emotionally and spiritually. When a person is sexually promiscuous, in a sense that person is joining his or her soul with the souls of others; besides being dishonouring to their own body, this promiscuity leads to confusion within their spirit and their emotions *(read 1 Corinthians 6:18)*. Whoever you join together with sexually, whether it is with a one-night stand, a long-term non-marital relationship, or with your husband, you become one with that person.

"Do you not know and realise that your bodies are members (bodily parts) of Christ (the Messiah)? Am I therefore to take the parts of Christ and make [them] parts of a prostitute? Never! Never! Or do you not know and realise that when a man joins himself to a prostitute, he becomes one body with her? The two, it is written, shall become one flesh" (1 Corinthians 6:15 TAB). It is for this reason why God requires us as single women to refrain from becoming sexually active with anyone apart from our own husbands. God

is not trying to cramp our style; rather, He is trying to save us from a life of misery, deceit, and total despair.

Many young women in our society try to paint the picture that all is well within their relationships. However, deep down some of them are empty and unfulfilled, giving out tirelessly and getting back nothing in return. For many of them there is no commitment in their cohabiting lifestyle, and therefore also no stability, with only a future of uncertainty hanging in the balance. Many give the impression that marriage is not important to them, when in reality they long with all their hearts for such a commitment.

As mature Christian singles our expectations are to be founded in and modelled by the Word of God. We may not be standing with the majority, but we will be standing side by side with the truth. The truth is what sets us apart from the crowd, and it is what makes us free. The book of *1 Corinthians* warns us to *"shun immorality and all sexual looseness [flee from impurity in thought, word, or deed]. Any other sin which a man commits is done outside the body, <u>but he who commits sexual immorality sins against his own body</u>" (1 Corinthians 6:18 TAB)*.

When a person turns from sin and becomes "born again," their body becomes the temple of God, and the Holy Spirit comes and lives within their spirit. That person is now changed and has a new way of thinking and therefore is not free to do as he/she pleases with his/her own body. They are not to treat it dishonourably anymore, but rather they are to honour God with it and bring glory to

Him *(1 Corinthians 6:19-20)*. This scripture also clearly states what our bodies were and were not designed for. *"Food [is intended] for the stomach and the stomach for food, but God will finally end [the function of] both and bring them to nothing. <u>The body is not intended for sexual immorality</u>, but [is intended] for the Lord, and the Lord [is intended] for the body [to save, sanctify, and raise it again]" (1 Corinthians 6:13 TAB).*

Since God is the One who created us, and every detail about our lives is important to Him, it follows therefore that God would devise a means to channel the natural sexual desires He instilled into us as human beings. Regardless of how Hollywood portrays sex, God did not design sex to be dirty, cheap, or frivolous. Because God created us, He knows our weaknesses, and right from the beginning He recognised that it was not a good thing for Adam to be alone. *"Now the Lord God said, it is not good (sufficient, satisfactory) that the man should be alone; <u>I will make him a helper</u> (suitable, adapted, complementary) for him" (Genesis 2:18 TAB).*

God recognised that the type of loneliness Adam was experiencing was not the desire for a friend or a buddy. Had it been a loneliness of that nature, God would have created for Adam another male companion. However, Adam's loneliness stemmed from an intimate need for a soul mate, and it was for that reason why God created him another human being, **of the opposite sex**, to compliment him and fill the void that he was experiencing. It is also for this reason that, as Christians, we believe God did not design two individuals of the same sex to derive pleasure from each other sexually and intimately.

It is clear from this verse in Genesis that God made Adam and Eve – not Adam and Steve or Eve and Jane. God knew that Adam and Eve would at some point be sexually attracted to each other. He did not ignore this factor, but provided an appropriate lifestyle for them so that mankind could fulfil these desires in a way that is pleasing and morally acceptable to Him — that lifestyle being known as monogamous, heterosexual marriage.

Contrary to what Satan wants us to believe about God, God is not old-fashioned, unfair, or insensitive. As mature single women you may feel that you do not always cope with your feelings as well as you should do in this area. However, don't allow Satan to condemn you. God has already given us a promise in *Romans 8:1: "Therefore, [there is] now no condemnation (no adjudging guilty of wrong) for those who are in Christ Jesus, who live [and] walk not after the dictates of the flesh, but after the dictates of the Spirit" (TAB).*

Rather than allowing Satan to tempt us beyond what we could bear, God provided us with the concept of marriage. We are shown in 1 Corinthians 7:2 that to avoid sexual immorality a man should have his **"own wife"** and a woman should have her **"own husband."** Further down in verses 7-8 of chapter 7, Paul tries to persuade the Corinthians that it might be to their advantage if they lived a life of celibacy and remained single like him. However, he quickly followed this statement with the reality that not everyone will want to remain celibate indefinitely, and he went on to encourage them that *"if they have not self-control (restraint of their passions), they should marry. For it is better to marry than to be aflame [with passion and tortured continually with ungratified desire]" (1 Corinthians 7:9 TAB)*. Note, however, that Paul realised some would have a desire to be sexually intimate, so he reminded them of their God-given obligations and that the right route was to be **joined together as one in holy matrimony.**

So how do we raise our expectations and our worth as mature Christian singles in this day and age? We live by God's Word and His Word alone. We do not allow society to set the pace with regard to our relationships, but we set the standard based on the Word of God. We put off the carnal desires and seek God's best for our lives. We let the men we are in relationships with know that we will not "give up the goods" whilst we are single. We will wait, however long it takes, for God's best.

And what kind of man is God's best for us? He is a man who will not try to seduce us into doing anything contrary to God's Word; he will be a man after God's own heart; he will know the Word and live by it; he is a man who will respect you as an individual – a man who knows that to ask you to be intimate with him outside of wedlock is to dishonour you and your body. Ladies, let's also be aware, sad though it is to say, that not every guy sitting in church will be all that he purports to be. There are some guys — well, let's expose them for what they really are, which is players — who will infiltrate themselves amongst the Christian crowd, and these players can come in all sorts of shapes and sizes, can be young and old, and also be mature or immature in the faith. As singles we need to wait on God for what I call "references" in connection to any potential partner when establishing new relationships. We need to check his references by asking questions such as, "Who is this new guy that has just come into the church?" "Where did he come from?" "What is his background?" Similar to when we apply for a job, any new employer will ask for references from your previous employers; after all, the new employer only has your CV (resume) and your word to go by in making an assessment of you at the interview. In order to consider whether you are the right person for the job, they will therefore rely heavily on those professional references and your past track record and recommendations.

They will especially be interested in knowing whether or not you are trustworthy, and how you cope in difficult situations. What your potential employer is trying to do is build a clearer picture of who you are, which is not always apparent at face value.

I'll share a personal story that highlights what I mean. I was once responsible for overseeing a small section of ladies and would often have to interview people with a view to taking on new employees. A particular young lady I recommended to my employers seemed, at face value, to be a great candidate for the job. She seemed extremely conscientious and hard working. At the time she was first employed, I was having problems with contacting her previous employers in trying to get a professional reference on her. It seemed that all my letters and telephone calls were going unanswered; however, I constantly kept trying to secure this reference. In the meantime, about a few months after this young girl had started working at our office, things started to go missing. At first it was just little things, but eventually the items started getting bigger, and a few of the senior partners found that money and a wallet went missing from their jackets. Eventually some laptops also went missing. I started to get a bit suspicious of this young woman for two reasons. Firstly, before she started, nothing of this sort had happened and secondly, as she did the filing, she was the only one who would go in and out of the partners' offices freely and therefore had complete access to their personal belongings. To cut a long story short, I confronted her and she admitted that she was the guilty party. When she finally left, I was able to eventually get through to her previous employer, only to find out that they were avoiding talking with me because she had done the exact same thing at their offices.

I used to believe that I was a good judge of character, but God has allowed a few individuals into my life over the years, both male and female, who have personified the saying "all that glitters is not gold," and it is for this reason, ladies, that I believe we should not be naïve in thinking that such individuals do not operate within the church and that every Christian man you meet will act in a way that honours you. Not all men who come across as "spiritual" really are. Therefore, ladies, let's guard our hearts against such individuals, because Satan is no respecter of persons, and he will operate through anyone who has given him an open invitation into their lives. And yes, they will seem genuine, because "players" can be to a certain extent – remember, they have been at this business for a long time, and because no one checks their "references," they continue to get away with unacceptable behaviour. If you let them into your life they will eventually, inevitably, break your heart and give you some sob story, because even they can't "play the game" for too long (It must be exhausting!), and eventually their past will start to catch up with them. Therefore, don't beat up on yourselves if you've gotten involved with any of these types, and please understand that their rejection of you is never about you, but is about their inability to commit to any one person at any one time. So ladies, if for some reason you may have let your guard down in this area, don't think that you can't restore your intimacy with God, because you can. Continue to hold your head up high, because after all, you are a woman of excellence. Remember that God's best man for you will not deceive you or expect you to do something you know is against His will.

Chapter Twelve

DID YOU KNOW THAT FALSE PERCEPTION CAN LEAD TO DECEPTION?

"For the vision is yet for an appointed time and it hastens to the end [fulfillment]; <u>it will not deceive or disappoint</u>. Though it tarry, wait [earnestly] for it, because it will surely come; it will not be behind-hand on its appointed day" (Habakkuk 2:3 TAB).

This is an area where as mature singles we can sometimes fall short. So often we have dreams and visions for our future which on the surface may seem to be legitimate and harmless; however, having the false perception that an idea or feeling is God's leading is often self-deception on our part. It is important that we learn to recognise God's voice in every area of our lives. It is not God's will for us to be deceived or disappointed by just any random "impression" that pops into our minds throughout our lives. Instead, His will is that at all times we have a level of discernment whereby we can know the voice of God versus our own desires.

God has a definite, specific, plan for your life when it comes to introducing you to your future husband. However, at times we have our own ideas and somehow think that if we can just help God along, then we will get to our mate that much quicker. Ladies, this is a big mistake. God does not need our help in this area; He is in total control. And that means that He works all things together for good. *"We are assured and know that [God being a partner in their labour) all things work together and are [fitting into a plan] for good to and for those who love God and are called according to [His] design and purpose" (Romans 8:28 TAB).*

This is an area where I believe God is still working on me. I have loved and lost; I have had impressions, ideas, visions – you name it, I've had it. But not one of these has led me to my future husband. They have just led to paths of embarrassment, shame, deception, and disappointment on my part. Having said all that, however, I do try my best to be obedient to God. Therefore I would never harbour anger or resentment against God or even myself when things do not turn out the way I had expected them to. My eyes have really been opened as to how easily our emotions can deceive us. I have also learned that Satan can listen in on some of our more intimate moments with God and run ahead of God to set in motion his counterfeit plans. That is why praying in the spirit is a good principle to adopt. When that "scrambler" gets turned on, Satan really is in trouble then, because he doesn't have a clue what you or I are praying about. And also remember that when you pray in the spirit you are praying God's perfect will for your life.

The reason I confess that God is still working on me is because I don't believe I have passed the examination in this area of my life, meaning, my ability to totally trust God, to wait on Him, and to not run off with vague impressions, but instead to simply wait for His specific purposes and will for my life. And until I do pass this test, I will just have to keep taking the exam over and over again until I achieve a passing score, so to speak! Then when I have finally passed, I know I will be ready for promotion to the next level that God has prepared for me.

This analogy is also true in our day-to-day lives. Can you remember what it was like at school, college or university, when there was a particular subject that you wanted to pass? Remember how you spent long hours preparing and studying so that you would be equipped to go into that examination room and ace the test? And it didn't matter how well you did on that paper, because if you got one mark less than the required pass mark – do you remember what they wrote on your paper? – That's right, "FAILED." The only way forward, then, was to go back to the books, revise your study methods extensively, and give it another shot until you passed.

As singles, I want you to know that sometimes you will fail in the area of love. And as I am talking to mature singles, I am sure you have some of your own stories to tell. Guess what? You won't always get the one that you **thought** you wanted, and there are so many reasons why that is so, all of which you will thank God for repeatedly when you finally get the right one. Ask most married couples and they'll tell you that the person they eventually married was not the first and only person they fell in love with. Just because you have made mistakes in the past in this area does not mean you should allow Satan to keep you locked up in the past. Go again, have another attempt at the exam. There is no shame in taking risks. Risks are what dreams are made of. You cannot allow fear to paralyse you from developing future relationships. At the appointed time, the right one will come into your life, and then you will be so glad you waited on God.

There is a wonderful scripture which gives us hope for the future during those times when we feel disappointed and let down: *"We are hedged in (pressed) on every side [troubled and oppressed in every way], but not cramped or crushed; <u>we suffer embarrassments</u> and are perplexed and unable to find a way out, but not driven to despair. We are pursued (persecuted and hard driven), but not deserted (to stand alone); we are struck down to the ground, <u>but never struck out and destroyed</u>" (2 Corinthians 4:8-9 TAB).*

Some situations in life may seem to crush us, and we might even suffer embarrassment as a result of our actions, but the key is to get up and keep going. As Christians we are not meant to stay down, wallowing in our own little pity party, but rather be continually having a praise party. <u>Praise God</u> for what you did not see, but for what He showed you. <u>Praise God</u> that He didn't allow you to marry the wrong person. <u>Praise God</u> because your future husband is still on the horizon. And the praises can go on and on and on – <u>Praise God</u>!

As I said earlier, God is still working on me in this area. He is chiselling the bits that will hinder my spiritual, emotional, and physical growth, and because of this, I have to be eternally grateful. God loves us so much and wants the best for us. His plans are to give us hope and a future *(Jeremiah 29:11)*. And we have to be willing to lay aside our ideas, goals, and dreams in exchange for the glorious plan He has for our lives.

Another way we can be deceived is when we take hold of specific scriptures and then stand on them to reinforce what we assume God has said to us in a particular situation. Whilst God's Word is based on truth, and in *Isaiah 55:11* it talks about *"His Word not returning to Him unaccomplished,"* we can, however, interpret scripture out of context.

Let me show you what I mean. For my own part, I believed I had received a specific word concerning a particular man I was attracted to. It came at a time in my life when I was not looking for anyone, and because I had done nothing to initiate this man's compliments, I was sure he must have come from God. However, Satan must have already intercepted my private petitions to God and thought he would set me up good and proper by distracting me off the path God has for me. In Dr. Don Raunikar's book, *Choosing God's Best*,[1] he has a chapter entitled "Recognising God's Voice" in which he gives a word of warning. He states, "... *the minute you start to specify how you want to hear from God - such as "putting out a fleece" – you open up yourself to being deceived by the enemy, who also speaks in the same spiritual sphere and dimension as the voice of the Holy Spirit ...*"

Knowing my track record of being attracted to particular men, only to have it come to nothing but eventually lead to disappointment at a later stage, I proceeded to tread very, very carefully from then on. I tried — oh, I tried very hard — to stay focused on God and to listen to His voice throughout this time. However, the clear word I kept receiving within my spirit was to wait, and so I took heed to that word and waited. Also during this time of trying to decipher between the voice of God and the voice of my desires, I received various scriptures that I thought were relevant and appropriate to my situation, and so I stood on them and, of course, comforted myself with them too. After all, when you have a verse of scripture, you're sure that gives it God's seal of approval, right? Oh, how wrong we can be, the result of which can be a false perception eventually leading to deception.

Looking back on it now, one of the scriptures I received was the opening one used in this chapter, that of Habakkuk 2:2-3. I kept on quoting to myself, "This vision that God has given me is for an appointed time;" "And I know I have not received the manifestations of it yet, but it will surely come;" "It will not deceive or disappoint me when it comes to fruition." That along with other scriptures was what I stood on to reinforce my "God-given vision" for my future mate.

Throughout this time I did not get any tangible evidence that this man was attracted to me and that alone should have sounded alarm bells in my spirit. I did, however, receive a few compliments from him now and then, which I naively took and ran with "up the aisle" in my imaginations, along with the bridal party, minister, photographer, the full works! Also — and I suppose this should have been a big eye opener — he did not pursue me in the way a person does when they are attracted to someone. Neither did he give me any indication that would even hint at these feelings. But I continued to believe in my heart that the "impression" I received was from God and that I was to exercise "my faith." I was sure that God would change "this" and God could change "that" and so on. Guess what — it was not to be. I eventually woke up and "smelt the coffee" – and of course found it to be totally charred. That perception that I held on to turned out to be false and it led to my imaginations and emotions deceiving me in a big way.

Of course the scriptures I was standing on were true, but they did not relate to that particular person or situation. If God's Word in Habakkuk 2:3 states that the vision He gives me will not deceive or disappoint me, then any vision I receive which does just that is not from God. I had to admit to myself that

I had missed the mark on this occasion, and then I had to ask for God's forgiveness and move forward. What I am pleased about, however, is that I did not make a complete fool of myself, and I continued to listen to that "wait" word that I **had** received from God along the way. That word saved me a lot of embarrassment and allowed my dignity and integrity to remain intact to this day. That man is now married and my friendship with him has not been affected in any way, and with no ill feelings on my part; in fact, I believe he did not even suspect a thing throughout the whole experience. Oh how gracious God is with our mistakes! Thank you, Lord.

Life is a learning process, and we need to appreciate that every experience we encounter is an experience that we can learn from. We can also recognise that when we see ourselves going down a similar path again, the alarm bells should go off in our spirit reminding us that we have already gone down that path and hopefully have learnt from our past mistakes.

I believe I am not alone in this area and that some of you too have learnt valuable lessons in the lost loves from your own lives. Guess what?! It is okay to admit that we did not hear God correctly or that we misinterpreted something He said to us. We are humans after all. I believe it is better to be honest with ourselves in this area than to dig ourselves deeper into a hole that we won't back out of because of our pride. Once God reveals the truth to us, the truth is liberating and freeing. And it is this very truth that will keep us from walking in pride. Pride is when an individual continues down a road, even when they know it is wrong, but will not acknowledge that they are in the wrong. And once God has dealt with any false perception that may have led to deception in our lives, it is with confidence that we can go on to the next level in God.

"Behold, I am doing a <u>new thing</u>! Now it springs forth; do you not perceive and know it and will you not give heed to it? I will even make a way in the wilderness and rivers in the desert" (Isaiah 43:19 TAB).

"Behold, the former things have come to pass, and <u>new things</u> I now declare; before they spring forth I tell you of them" (Isaiah 42:9 TAB).

A new day is coming. That is why I am so excited to share the next chapter with you — because I do believe that for every 'Ruth' there is a 'Boaz.' And where doors have been shut, God, **and only God**, can open them.

Chapter Thirteen

FOR EVERY 'RUTH' THERE IS A 'BOAZ'

"And my <u>God will liberally supply</u> (fill to the full) <u>your every need</u> according to His riches in glory in Christ Jesus" *(Philippians 4:19 TAB).*

I strongly believe that God has ordained a specific plan for your life. We have learnt this from previous chapters as revealed to us in *Jeremiah 29: 11-14*. I also believe that God is divinely leading you in the direction of your future husband without you being aware of His handiwork (because that is how God likes to do things – with Him being in control and not us).

We also know from His Word that He will not withhold that which is good from us as long as we continue to walk uprightly *(Psalm 84:11)*. Therefore, we are to strive to make Him the Number One priority of our lives by continually seeking Him first and His kingdom. After such a commitment, we are guaranteed that all 'other things' will be added to our lives. *"But seek (aim at and strive after) first of all His kingdom and His righteousness (His way of doing and being right), and then all these things taken together will be given you besides" (Matthew 6:33 TAB).*

I want you to look at the book of Ruth with me, which begins with the story of Naomi and Elimelech and their two sons. This family leaves the confines of their home in Bethlehem-Judea (House of Bread) because of a severe famine, and they settle in the land of Moab. Whilst as inhabitants there, the two sons choose wives for themselves from the Moabite women, whose names were Orpah and Ruth. Whilst they dwelt in the land of Moab, Naomi's husband died, followed shortly by her two sons. The three women now shared a common ground; they were all widows. No doubt they helped each other through what must have been a very emotional time. The Bible speaks compassionately about caring for widows: *"[Always] treat with great consideration and give aid to those who are truly widowed (solitary and without support). But if a widow has children or grandchildren, see to it that these are first made to understand that it is their religious duty [to defray their natural obligation to those] at home, and make return to their parents or grandparents [for all their care by contributing to their maintenance], for this is acceptable in the sight of God] (1 Timothy 5:3-4 TAB).*

If you know someone who has recently become a widow, it is your duty to minister effectively to her. I have heard a number of widowed women say that the worse thing a person can do at such a time is to ignore them. Because of the unfortunate fact that they now do not have a husband, the social invitations seem to stop coming altogether, and many times they are left feeling isolated and disheartened. Sometimes silence is not golden, and these women need to know that you will be there for them, even if it is just to listen to them reminisce over the past. *Verse 5* gives the widow the greatest comfort that she will experience throughout her time of being alone again, the fact that God will not forsake her. *"Now [a woman] who is a real widow and is left entirely alone and desolate has fixed her hope on God and perseveres in supplications and prayers night and day" (1 Timothy 5:5 TAB).*

Despite her widowhood, Naomi knew the comfort of having a relationship with Jehovah-Jireh (our God who provides) and that she could draw on His strength. Ruth and Orpah only knew their foreign gods, but because of their association with Naomi, they too experienced God's comfort as they came under the umbrella of Naomi's protection. That is the beauty of the power of association. It is not always 'what you know,' but sometimes it is 'who you know.'

Naomi decided to return home to Bethlehem-Judea, as she learnt that the famine had lifted and God had indeed revisited His people. When Naomi and her family left Bethlehem-Judea in the first instance, they were effectively turning their backs on the "House of Bread/House of Praise." They must not have realised that regardless of how severe the famine in Bethlehem-Judea was, God would have provided for them as a family. In your own single state, your circumstances may look dire, and it may appear like you are never going to get married, but do not jump ship. You don't know what is around the corner. God will always provide for His people when they stay in the confines of His protection.

Therefore, do not go outside the confines of the "House of Bread" (Christendom) and escape to "Moab" (the world) to look for your mate. It may look as if there is a shortage of men within the House of Bread, but trust God and wait for His provision. With the benefit of hindsight (wisdom after the event), I wonder if things would have turned out differently for Naomi and her family had she stayed and waited in Bethlehem-Judea. However, with all that Naomi experienced, she is not the same person coming out of Moab as she had been going in. She is leaving Moab as a childless widow with only two daughters-in-law to show for her time spent living in his city.

It would appear that Naomi had a good relationship with Ruth and Orpah, and when they heard that she was leaving, they expressed a great desire to go with her. Naomi assured them that it was in their best interest if they stayed in their own country, as they would have a better chance of remarrying. She had nothing to offer them and they would be leaving all they had to go back with her. And Naomi too was unsure what awaited her when she returned to Bethlehem. Whilst Orpah took the advice of Naomi and kissed her and bade her farewell, Ruth was not so convinced.

Being married to Naomi's son and having become her daughter-in-law, Ruth would have been influenced by their lifestyle and seen their devotion to their God. Weighing this against what she had been accustomed to before her marriage to Naomi's son, perhaps Ruth saw this as her opportunity to make a new life for herself and to separate herself from what she knew to be ungodly. *"Therefore if any person is [ingrafted] in Christ (the Messiah) he is a new creation (a new creature altogether); the old [previous moral and spiritual condition] has passed away. Behold the fresh and new has come!" (2 Corinthians 5:17 TAB)* Ruth was becoming a new creation, and by leaving Moab and heading for new pastures in Bethlehem-Judah, the House of Bread where God provides, she was saying goodbye to her old lifestyle and embracing a new way of living.

Ruth's devotion to Naomi is remarkable and her declaration of faith is one of great commitment: *"Entreat me not to leave thee, or to return from following after thee: for whither thou goest, I will go; and where thou lodgest, I will lodge: thy people shall be my people, and thy God my God: Where thou diest, will I die, and there will I be buried: the Lord do so to me, and more also, if ought but death part thee and me" (Ruth 1:16-17 KJV).*

Ruth was determined and her mind was made up. She wanted to go with Naomi regardless of what the future outcome would be. She wanted Naomi's people to become her people. And she longed for Naomi's God to be her God.

When we accept Jesus Christ as our Lord and Saviour, like Ruth we make a declaration to the world. We renounce our sins through repentance. We turn and walk in a new direction. We declare that we have turned our back on sin and will now walk in righteousness, pursuing a relationship with God. *(See Romans 10:8-10)*. This decision causes us to become a new creature in Christ as we reject the old and embrace the new.

Naomi recognised from the change in Ruth's attitude that something had taken place in her life and did not try to deter her from returning with her to Bethlehem-Judah, but welcomed her company. And on that note they left Moab, with Ruth turning her back on everything she had ever known to face a future with the God of the Israelites.

On arrival at their destination, there was no time to waste. With no male figure around the house, these two women had to act promptly if they were to survive. They arrived at an appropriate time, as it was the beginning of the barley harvest. Characteristic of Ruth's nature, she offered to go out and work. Naomi gave Ruth the go-ahead and the necessary advice on the areas that were safest to work. And characteristic with our Father's nature, Ruth is providentially led to work in the field of her future husband, Boaz, who also is a direct descendent of Naomi's. Just imagine the timing of this event. Ruth could have chosen any field to work in, but God was divinely leading this young lady, who had put her life into His care when she decided to accept Him as her God. *Psalm 37:3* encourages us to *"Trust in the Lord, and do good; so shall thou dwell in the land, and verily thou shalt be fed" (KJV)*. God saw Ruth's faithfulness to her mother-in-law and to Him, and He was going to see to it that Ruth was rewarded for the good choices she had made for her life.

God is not a respecter of persons. God too will guide our footsteps when we are to meet our future partners. He will providentially work all circumstances for our good, ensuring we are in the right place at the right time. In the amplified version of *Psalm 37:23-24* it reminds us that *"The steps of a [good] man (or woman in our case) are directed and established by the Lord when He delights in his way [and He busies Himself with his every step]. Though he falls, he shall not be utterly cast down, for the Lord grasps his hand in support and upholds him."* Even at times when we miss the mark, He is mindful of this fact and is ready to pick us up and put us back on track. He is the God of second chances. Through Him blessing the life of Ruth and Boaz, Naomi was also in line to receive His favour a second time round.

As Ruth gleaned in the field of a wealthy man by the name of Boaz, this man, being her future husband, noticed her hard work. A note for you ladies: your future husband will admire you from afar without your prior knowledge. He will make enquiries as to who you are out of interest for you. Boaz enquired as to who Ruth was. There was something different about the way she conducted herself which got her noticed. (I can imagine at this particular time that Ruth did not look her best either. She probably had her work clothes on and I bet she was working without the aid of make-up too. Nevertheless, she got noticed.) Ladies, our work will always speak for us. We do not have to try and pull anyone down to get to the top. Nor do we have to cheat or manipulate our colleagues to get a promotion; God will bring us before great men. *Proverbs 18:16 teaches us that "A man's gift maketh room for him, and bringeth him before great men" (KJV).* We are also encouraged that our promotion comes from God. He is the one who promotes us. *"For promotion cometh neither from the east, nor from the west, nor from the south. But God is the judge: He putteth down one, and setteth up another" (Psalm 74: 6-7 KJV).*

Ruth found favour in Boaz's eyes. She did not physically do anything to get his attention (remember she was in her work clothes) and certainly was not intentionally trying to impress anyone. She was simply doing her work with excellence and was not aware that she was being "checked out." We can be encouraged in our singleness as we observe Ruth, who may not have been mature in age, but all the same was a unique lady who possessed special inner qualities. She obviously was not like other Moabite women. Her warm and kind nature is probably what had attracted Mahlon (Naomi's son) to take her for a wife in the first place, even though it meant that he would not be marrying an Israelite woman.

Ruth worked hard all day, and because she found favour in the eyes of Boaz, he gave instructions to his servants that they were to drop extra bundles of wheat so that she could glean these as well. He also instructed Ruth to stay with his reapers and not to consider going to another field, but that she was welcome to follow his reapers to whichever field they went to and reap there. I am sure you will agree that for a foreigner in a land she knew nothing about, this definitely was divine favour and the hand of the Almighty God. To cut a long story short, Ruth got her man. And they lived happily ever after [for the full impact of this love story, I recommend that you read the book of Ruth for yourself].

Pause for a moment and think. In your pursuit of finding your soul mate, where is God taking you? And to whose path is He leading you? Sometimes we get so frustrated in our wait that we fail to recognise who we are waiting with — the Omniscient God who knows everything, including the end of the story, so to speak. But yet still we get anxious, trying to make signs and often nudging God, impatiently stating, "He is over there, God! That's the one I want." God already knows who you want, but He knows who is best for you too. And you can bet that if the one **you** want is not the one **He** wants, your loving God will not allow that connection to be made, unless you take matters into your hands and thereby, of your own free will, force God's hand. So just chill and enjoy yourselves. It is better to wait with peace and serenity until God providentially sets things in motion. And trust me, He is an awesome God. He has been in the matchmaking business since the beginning of time and hasn't once gotten it wrong.

And remember too that it is better to be in God's perfect will than to be in His permissive will. Yes, I know it might seem hard to wait when you see nothing good happening, but it will be well worth the wait. Your 'Boaz' is just around the corner, but wait for God's divine direction and you will not be disappointed. He is more excited to give you your 'Boaz' than you are to receive him, because He delights in His children and only wants the best for us. But before your 'Boaz' comes along, allow God to use your singleness to give you insight as to the type of wife He wants you to be. Try taking a leaf out of Proverbs 31, commonly called "the woman's book of the Bible," because when you marry your soul mate, you will be glad you did.

Chapter Fourteen

TAKE A LEAF OUT OF THE BOOK OF 'MRS. PROVERBS 31'

"He who finds a [true] wife finds a good thing and obtains favour from the Lord"
(Proverbs 18:22 TAB).

The woman described throughout Proverbs 31 has been characterised as the "superwoman" of the Bible. However, as mature singles with a future desire to be a wife and perhaps a mother, there is much that we can learn from the qualities that this woman uses to ensure that her household is adequately nurtured and cared for.

Proverbs 31:10 unfolds by asking the question *"A capable, intelligent, and virtuous woman – <u>who is he who can find her</u>? She is far more precious than jewels and her value is far above rubies or pearls"* *(TAB)*. This is the standard that godly men who are seeking God for a wife should be looking for – a capable, intelligent, and virtuous woman. All of these are qualities which you will have the opportunity to develop whilst you are single, therefore you should value this time and use it wisely. Such a woman's worth goes far beyond that of the most delicate and expensive piece of exquisite jewellery.

Proverbs 12:4 goes on to describe additional qualities of a virtuous woman: *"A virtuous and worthy wife [earnest and strong in character] is a crowning joy to her husband, but she who makes him ashamed is as rottenness in his bones" (TAB)*. I believe that the majority of men are looking for someone who will be able to compliment them, someone they can show off and who they know will not embarrass them in public or in front of their family and friends. *"Her husband is greatly respected when he deliberates with the city fathers" (Proverbs 31:23 TM)*. The opposite of the virtuous woman would be the woman who brings shame to her husband and disrespects his self-worth. In *Proverbs 27:15*, The Message translation spares no punches, but delivers it quite plain and clear for all to heed: *"A nagging spouse is like the drip, drip, drip of a leaky faucet; You can't turn it off, and you can't get away from it."* You may smile, but that is how serious it can get. Nonetheless, that is not the leaf that we should want to take out of this book, so it is wise that we start learning to possess the fruit of the spirit as given to us in *Galatians 5:22-23*. When we work on our love, joy, peace, patience, an even-temper (forbearance), kindness, goodness, faithfulness, gentleness and self-control, we will become the kind of wives God has designed us to be.

"Houses and riches are the inheritance from fathers, but a wise, understanding, and prudent wife is from the Lord" (Proverbs 19:14 TAB). Remember how Job's wife discouraged him and offered no support to him at the one point in his life when he really needed her to stand with him? *(See Job 2: 9-10).* Job rebuked her and told her that she spoke "foolishly." She obviously was not wise, and she did not act prudently and supportive when she was required to do so, and thus she lost the respect of her husband.

Getting back to our "Proverbs 31 woman," *verses 11-12* show us what her husband thinks of her: *"The heart of her husband trusts in her confidently and relies on and believes in her security, so that he has no lack of [honest] gain or need of [dishonest] spoil. She comforts, encourages, and does him only good as long as there is life within her" (TAB).* Are you trustworthy? Can you be relied upon? These are just some of the issues that will arise in your marriage, and your husband will want to know that he can believe in you and that he will have no cause to doubt your integrity. The way we live our single lives will determine what type of marriage material we will produce. This God-given time as a mature single should be used as a stepping stone to catapult us into our future destiny.

Marriage will not always be a bed of roses, and there will be times when your husband will be looking to you for comfort and encouragement. This couple in Proverbs 31 obviously had a very loving relationship, because he rests confidently in his wife's ability to be there for him. Singles, we have to learn how to be able to comfort our mate, be there for him, and know how to stand by our man in his time of need. Are you ready to be that committed? This is one of the factors that we must consider when desiring to walk down the aisle and commit ourselves to a lifelong marriage relationship.

From *verses 13-15* we learn that she is not an idle person when it comes to providing for her household, but rather is diligent. She is up before dawn, working with her hands. She shops around for the best bargains and provides nutritious and wholesome meals for her husband and children. As single women, this may be something that will be new to us. We are probably used to organising our day around ourselves. For so long the theme of our life is "me, myself, and I," and then it becomes "we." We therefore will have to develop our interaction skills so that we can prioritise our day, balancing all the various jobs that will require accomplishing.

Our Proverbs 31 woman also has a head for business *(verses 16-22)* and ensures that her roles do not conflict with one another. She does not allow her career to stand in the way of her godly duties as a wife and a mother. Just by reading the account of *Proverbs 31:10-31*, we can see that this is an extraordinary woman, for she also makes coverlets, cushions, and rugs of tapestry. Now I am not suggesting that you go out and buy a sewing machine and struggle to do all of these things, because everyone is different and we all have our own strengths and weaknesses. I believe at this stage in our lives, however, that we should know our God-given gifts and what it is that we are good at, and therefore strive to excel in those areas in order to be a blessing in our future homes.

Also, this woman's appearance is important to her; therefore, she does not neglect it *(verse 22)*. Her clothing is of pure and fine linen – a woman of class, only the best, of course. If your appearance is important to you now and you take great care of it whilst you are single, then when you get married there is no need to let yourself go. Your husband most likely will be attracted to your looks and the way you take care of yourself, and he deserves this look to be maintained. [Revisit Chapter 7 about pampering yourself.] *"Even though strength and dignity are her clothing, her position is strong and secure. She rejoices over the future [the latter day or time to come, knowing that she and her family are in readiness for it!]" (Proverbs 31:25-26 TAB).*

Finally, as a woman of excellence, she makes herself available spiritually. *"She opens her mouth in skilful and godly wisdom, and on her tongue is the law of kindness [giving counsel and instruction]. She looks well to how things go in her household, and the bread of idleness (gossip, discontent, and self-pity) she will not eat" (verses 26-27 TAB).* Titus 2:5 defines the guidelines of how a godly wife should behave: *"To be self-controlled, chaste, homemakers, good-natured (kind-hearted), adapting and subordinating themselves to their husbands, that the word of God may not be exposed to reproach (blasphemed or discredited)" (TAB)*. So as we learn from the principles of the "Proverbs 31 woman," we can see that we are not to be partakers in the bread of idleness and gossiping, which only eats away at our valuable time which could be better used serving our husbands and looking after our children.

The Bible is entwined with stories of various types of wives[1] and their natures. The stories would be good for us to study and review so that we can see the attitudes we should either adopt or drop:

A) Disobedient Eve *(Genesis 3:1-8)*
B) Obedient Sarah *(1 Peter 3:5-6)*
C) Lot's worldly wife – whose name did not even get a mention *(Genesis 19:26)*
D) Manoah's humble wife *(Judges 12:22-23)*
E) Prayerful Hannah *(1 Samuel 1:1-15)*
F) Prudent Abigail *(1 Samuel 25:3, 14-35)*
G) Criticising Michal *(2 Samuel 6:15-16)*
H) The Unscrupulous Jezebel *(1 King 21:5-15)*
I) Modest Vashti *(Esther 1:11-12)*
J) Job's Foolish Wife – who, like Lot's wife, did not get her name mentioned *(Job 2:7-10)*
K) Cruel Herodias *(Matthew 14:3-12)*
L) Righteous Elisabeth *(Luke 1:5-6)*
M) Lying Sapphira *(Acts 5:1-10)*

Eve was the first wife recorded in the Bible, and she was designed to be a helpmeet for Adam *(Genesis 2:18, 20)*. From the above descriptions, it is clear that a woman can be a help to a man or a hindrance to him. Have you thought about what kind of wife you will be? What qualities do you have that will contribute to your husband's well being? The opening scripture reminds us again that *"Whoso findeth a wife findeth a good thing, and obtaineth favour of the Lord" (Proverbs 18:22 KJV).*

The choice is left to you as to what kind of wife you will be. However, the principles of the "Proverbs 31 woman" are God's ideal for us. *"Her children respect and bless her; her husband joins in with words of praise: Many women have done wonderful things, but you've outclassed them all! Charm can mislead and beauty soon fades. The woman to be admired and praised is the woman who lives in the Fear of God. Give her everything she deserves! Festoon her life with praises!" (Proverbs 31:28-31 TM).*

Now that's the kind of wife you should emulate, the "Proverbs 31 woman" – God's ideal choice. However, I wonder what the men's perspectives are for a godly wife? The next chapter should offer some insightful tips on what is their position on the subject and what they are looking for in a future potential mate.

CHAPTER FIFTEEN

BY THE WAY, WHAT ARE THE MEN DOING?

"Now the Lord God said, it is not good (sufficient, satisfactory) that the man should be alone; I will make him a help meet (suitable, adapted, complementary) for him"
(Genesis 2:18 TAB).

I suppose it is fair to say that this book would not be complete without getting a male perspective on why many men also remain single well into their 30s and beyond. So I've sought to look at the topic of being a mature single from the men's perspective, to help us gain insight into the male psyche. So ladies, before we get tough on the brothers, let's hear them out. Let's get their side of the story; after all, relationships aren't one-sided. From hearing their side of the story, I do believe that some of their reasons are valid and legitimate. I also believe that some of the men who delay marriage until their 30s or 40s have had an opportunity at some stage in their lives to be married, but perhaps due to circumstances, may have missed it and the opportunity hasn't yet presented itself again. Many of the men say they have a number of friends who are married, which enables them to observe the good, and perhaps bad, traits of those marriages. Therefore, their number one concern is that they hear from God 100% in choosing a wife and not be led by their own feelings. It is extremely important to the guys that when making a decision for their lifetime marriage partner that they are in the perfect will of God and not the permissive will of God. I will discuss this more in depth later in the chapter.

Often, some single ladies in the church will accuse the men of being scared and not wanting to make a commitment. However, we have to understand that from their perspective it is all about getting it right at the outset as to how the marriage will develop. Men are logical thinkers. They like things worked out. They need to know where they are. They need to be assured that they are making a 'God' choice as opposed to a 'good' choice. They meticulously need to have the I's dotted and the T's crossed. And this is not something that we should fault them on, because we want to know that when a man approaches us to make a marriage proposal, that he is serious and has every intention on following through with that commitment. So sisters, give the brothers time to work things out in their own minds and with God, and try not to pressure them. A number of guys have told me that some women come across as too needy, seeming desperate to get married. So ladies, bear that in mind and perhaps tone it down a little.

A word of advice, however, to the brothers reading this book; I would like to share something with you taken from the words of one of the wisest men recorded in Scripture (yes, a brother). In *Ecclesiastes 11:4*, Solomon says, *"He who observes the wind [and waits for all conditions to be favourable] will not sow, and he who regards the clouds will not reap" (TAB).* In today's language, that translates to "If you wait for perfect conditions, you will never get anything done." Guys, if you are waiting for "Miss Perfect," you will probably wait until Jesus returns, because she does not exist. And the guys should know this only too well because they are not presenting themselves as Mr. Perfect either. You know that you too come with your flaws. Sometimes as individuals we can have this perfect picture in our minds that stubbornly refuses to shift until we get someone who's very close to what we are looking for. Ladies, you know what I am talking about. The majority of women have on their checklist "tall, dark, and handsome." And for the guys, your list includes "great figures, stunning looks, long hair," etc. But let's be "real." How many of your friends do you know who actually got the picture they had originally painted? In reality, not many, right?! And those who were adamant and stuck to their original picture find themselves much older and possibly feeling unfulfilled, as their dream is now a living nightmare and not how they had quite imagined it. Guys! How do you think it makes some women feel when you go out looking with these specifications, often overlooking the bigger beautiful women with shorter hair who would make the perfect wife if given half the chance?! So give some of us a break and be real. You say you want to be led by God; well, God may challenge your thinking in this area, so be prepared for that to happen.

As I have previously said, men are forward planners. The majority of the time they like to weigh the pros and cons before going ahead and committing themselves to anything. And this is true whether they are choosing a new car, a new house, a job, and yes, even a wife. Ladies, this thinking, however, is biblical in its content, so try not to be too hard on the guys if they delay proposing. Jesus showed us that it is good to weigh situations when He posed this question regarding the cost of discipleship. *"For which of you, wishing to build a farm building, does not first sit down and calculate the cost [to see] whether he has sufficient means to finish it? Otherwise, when he has laid the foundation and is unable to complete [the building], all who see it will begin to mock and jeer at him. Saying, this man began to build and was not able (worth enough) to finish. Or what king, going out to engage in conflict with another king, will not first sit down and consider and take counsel whether he is able with ten thousand [men] to meet him who comes against him with twenty thousand? And if he cannot [do so], when the other king is still a great way off, he sends an envoy and asks the terms of the peace"* (Luke 14:28-32 TAB).

It can be said that this type of thinking is based not only on common sense, but also on "divine intervention" sense. Jesus also gave another example regarding the type of foundation a person builds on *(Matthew 7:24-27)*, highlighting that it is important how we build relationships and nurture the authenticity and depths of them (see chapter 10, "Square Pegs Don't Fit Into Round Holes").

In the natural, we can appreciate the importance of erecting a building on a good foundation. Regardless of how impressive the architect's plans are, the ultimate objective is for the building to be strong and functional, as well as a spectacular sight to behold. If the foundation is not laid correctly from the outset with precision and care, it is only a matter of time before that building, in all its splendour and glory will collapse into a heap of rubble. Likewise, marriages need to be established on a solid (and biblical) foundation from their inception. Therefore, the mature men will know only too well that there is more to marriage than just having someone who looks beautiful on the end of their arm.

Proverbs 18:22 gives men the assurance that when they find a wife, she will be a "good thing" and that they will "obtain favour from God." This would suggest that they are the ones who are to go looking for the woman and not vice versa. For some ladies, especially the mature ones that have been waiting around for a while, this might not go down too well in the 21st Century, but it is scriptural. And also, most guys I have spoken to say they do not like women to do the approaching, as they feel it usurps their authority. Therefore, ladies, always remember that men by nature are the hunters and we are to be the hunted. So try to stick to your feminine role and let the men fulfil their God–given, masculine role. They are looking for a woman to enhance their life, someone who will be to the man as a helpmeet, according to *Genesis 2:18: "Now the Lord God said, it is not good (sufficient, satisfactory) that the man should be alone; I will make him a helper meet (suitable, adapted, complementary) for him" (TAB).*

Ladies! Please re-read Chapter 14 of this book and see God's design for you and how you are to support your future mate. When God sends your future mate looking for you (to "hunt" you down), you should be ready to be found. That is why God has given you this special time to prepare yourself. Therefore, do not waste this time idly, feeling sorry for yourself because a man has not yet proposed to you. Instead utilise this time to reach your full potential in God and to be a blessing to that man when he comes into your life.

Another area that some guys have been honest about is their ability to be attracted to more than one woman at a time. It would seem that they have the upper hand in this respect, only due to the fact that in most Christian circles the sisters outnumber the brothers. This factor is borne in mind in their decision when choosing a mate, and the immature men often take advantage of the situation and think it is acceptable to date more than one woman at a time. I believe that those guys who are serious about making a commitment will channel their feelings and attractions more maturely and allow the Holy Spirit to do the leading and guiding at such an important juncture in their lives. These men will have respect for a woman's feelings and will have the wisdom not to make a commitment they cannot fulfil.

Personally, I am not attracted to the idea of dating men just for the sake of having someone to go out with or to be in a long-term relationship that is going nowhere. I would rather wait, however long, until a man knows he is interested in me as a prospective wife and then pursues me along those lines. Dating with no real future is only a waste of my time and his time, with the result being that you get a long list of failed relationships in your personal history, along with the hurts and disappointments they bring. I do not believe this is God's design for mature Christian singles. He has called us to be women of excellence and that should mean excellence in our relationships as well.

I believe that God has given men the mandate when looking for a wife. He has given them a godly blueprint found in His Word of what to look for. He has left them with no doubt as to the kind of wife they will be satisfied with, and I believe that they are actively seeking God in this area. I also believe He has given women a mandate too. And even though sometimes we might get anxious in our "wait," I believe He works all things together for our good *(Romans 8:28)*. God orders your steps, and He delights in every step that you take. With God, everything is governed by His timing. *Ecclesiastes 3* talks about in the seasons of our lives: a time to be born, and a time to die; a time to love, and a time to hate, and so on.

To answer the question, "What are the men doing?" I believe they are preparing themselves to be the best that God has called them to be, so that in turn they too will be all that we have prayed for them to be.

And ladies, whilst you wait for God to prepare the men, just remember that you will not be single forever, as this season too will pass.

CHAPTER SIXTEEN

THIS TOO WILL PASS

"For those who wait for the Lord [who expect, look for, and hope in Him] shall change and renew their strength and power, they shall lift their wings and mount up [close to God] as eagles [mount up to the sun]; they shall run and not be weary, they shall walk and not faint or become tired"
(Isaiah 40:31 TAB).

Have you ever had to wait on God for anything? How did it make you feel? As mature single women, whilst waiting and relying on God for a marriage partner, you learn to develop an inner strength that can only come from Him. You come to realise that you've got what it takes to be fulfilled and satisfied in today's society. Regardless of how you are made to feel, you get by, and why? Because God's Word is pregnant with promises for you to take hold of and personally claim as your very own: *"I waited patiently and expectantly for the Lord; <u>and he inclined to me and heard my cry</u>"* (Psalms 40:1 TAB). *"Wait on the Lord: be of good courage, <u>and He shall strengthen thine heart</u>: wait, I say, on the Lord"* (Psalm 27:14 KJV). *"My soul, wait thou only upon God; for <u>my expectation is from Him</u>"* (Psalm 62:5 KJV).

In our time of waiting on God in this particular area, I believe our obedience and faithfulness will come up before him as a memorial. There are many examples in the Bible of people who waited on God, and this time proved profitable in the long run. One such person was a man named Cornelius, whose story is found in the books of *Acts 10:1-4*. Cornelius was described as a devout man, a man who feared God and led his household in this same vein. He gave to charitable causes and prayed earnestly to God in faith. His devotion to God paid off; we read in verse 4 how the Lord visited him in a vision and revealed that He had seen the lifestyle Cornelius had led, and that what he had done had 'come up as a memorial' before God.

God is Omniscient; therefore, He is aware of every step that you embark on. When we know and understand God, it is easier for us to trust and wait on Him. *Habakkuk 2:3* confirms that there are appointed times for things to happen. *"For the vision is yet for an appointed time and it hastens to the end [fulfilment]; it will not deceive or disappoint. Though it tarry, wait [earnestly] for it, because it will surely come; it will not be behind-hand on its appointed day (TAB).*

It is important to realise that our life naturally consists of various seasons. Every season has a beginning and an end. *"To everything there is a season, and a time for every matter or purpose under heaven" (Ecclesiastes 3:1 TAB).* For those of us who have a desire to be married at some point in our lives, we can view our singleness as a temporary season which will eventually pass.

God will not only honour our faithfulness to Him, but He will give us the desires of our hearts. *Psalm 37:3-5* encourages us to *"Trust (lean on, rely on, and be confident) in the Lord and do good; so shall you dwell in the land and feed surely on His faithfulness, and truly you shall be fed. Delight yourself also in the Lord, <u>and He will give you the desires and secret petitions of your heart</u>. Commit your way to the Lord [roll and repose each care of your load on Him]; trust (lean on, rely on, and be confident) also in Him and He will bring it to pass" (TAB).* If we believe it, then it's a done deal. However, try not to waste your season as a single woman, but use it to prepare yourself for the next season you will enter into as a married woman. From talking to many married women, this transition is going to take a lot of hard work, commitment and a lot of re-adjusting on our part. Just imagine, no more cooking for one (and we know some of the dull uninteresting meals we can prepare for ourselves at times). We would now have another person to answer to. And even spending our hard earned cash, we would have to think twice about. So ladies, these are some of the things that as singles we are accustomed to, but will have to change.

Marriage is for life and is not for immature individuals. You have to be willing to take the rough with the smooth. Your life will drastically change and you have to be prepared for this. If you are not prepared to change just yet, then perhaps you need to stay single a bit longer and re-evaluate your life.

There are some married people who, in an attempt to spare singles from some of the heartaches that can go with the whole marriage package, try to encourage singles that they are better off in their present state. Sometimes I think that maybe these people have forgotten what it was like to be single, or perhaps they were never single for a long period of time. Also, some singles have physical feelings and desires for intimacy which are God-given. If it is better to remain single, what are they to do with these feelings? Therefore, marriage is a route that some singles will want to pursue. *1 Corinthians 7:9* shows us that these feelings are legitimate and that something should be done about them to stop singles falling into sin. *"But if they have not self-control (restraint of their passions), they should marry. For it is better to marry than to be aflame [with passion and tortured continually with ungratified desire]" (TAB).*

As 'mature' singles we are quite aware that there will be ups and downs in marriage, but that is true in life anyway. It is a fact that anything we embark on in this life will present its various challenges and experiences, but we do not give up on them because of what we fear. We press on. And especially as Christians, we look to God and trust in Him. We buy our houses, even though we know a mortgage is a great financial pressure to endure. We pursue careers, subjecting ourselves to tight deadlines and employee interaction within the work environment. Couples have children, even when they may not have the first clue about how to bring up a child or be good parents. And the list goes on and on. So I do believe that as mature singles we have taken into consideration that it is going to take commitment and hard work to make our marriages work and, with the help of God, this is something that we are prepared for, mentally, physically, and spiritually.

Also appreciate the fact that as a single woman in your thirties, and perhaps older, you have had the benefit of learning from the mistakes others have made. When I look back to my early twenties, I had a lot of friends who were getting married one after the other. One year I was invited to seventeen weddings (and I am not joking), all of which I went to apart from one. And even though those weddings were lovely and elaborate, it is sad to report, however, that most of those marriages today have ended in divorce. Some were too young; some were in love with the **idea** of marriage but not the reality of it. And the remaining marriages ended for various other reasons. In their defence, however, it would be fair to say that there was not as much teaching and books back then as there is today about marriage and relationships, and perhaps these marriages could have been salvaged had they received the appropriate counselling before it was too late.

Throughout my years of being single, I have been blessed to have heard the subject of marriage and relationships preached from the pulpit on a regular basis. I have been able to hear ministers share and be open about their marriages and the struggles they experienced in the earlier part of their marriages, so that others can avoid some of the pitfalls that they fell into through a lack of knowledge. Sometimes it's easy to make an assumption that others have this "great marriage" because of what we can perceive from the outward appearance. Therefore, we should be grateful for their willingness to open up to us, which can equip and challenge us to stretch our own thinking. I am not saying that we will not make mistakes when we eventually enter into marriage, but it is important to do your homework. If it means buying tapes, books or going to seminars/conferences, then avail yourselves of such edification. What you sow today will be what you reap tomorrow. You cannot afford to be laid back in this area and feel that everything will fall into place after the wedding day. The wedding day is the first day of the rest of your lives together as a married couple. There is a saying that should be a great eye opener for us single women, which is "to be forewarned is to be forearmed." By doing a bit of homework before you get married, it might just be the icing on the cake when you run into difficulties. Therefore, read the right books, listen to the relevant tapes, and allow God to prepare you to be a good helpmeet to your future husband.

Insightful Tips for the Unique "Mature" Single

As an encouragement to you all, I would like to have concluded this book with news that I had met someone and had gotten married, but that is not the case. A couple of years ago I did meet someone who I thought was special and who I felt quite positive about, especially as we had what I thought was a lot in common and enjoyed each other's company, but unfortunately the timing wasn't right. At the time he had a lot of issues going on in his life, and I was just another distraction, and so the relationship ended. If I were to be honest, I would have to say that the process of going through a failed relationship and feeling rejected wasn't easy, but you do with time learn to eventually let go emotionally and move on. I also learnt that developing relationships with the opposite sex can be hard work especially since we think so differently that it would seem like we are from different planets; I'm sure you know what I mean, with them being from Mars and us from Venus as John Gray's book would suggest. However, I do believe we can learn to appreciate each other's 'worlds' and get on with each other on a mutually amicable basis. Gary Chapman's book on *The Five Love Languages for Singles*[1] shares some interesting concepts of ways for enhancing our relationships between the sexes.

In closing, I sometimes like to compare my life with friends I grew up with, if only to see what paths we have taken that were different. I am amazed by the diversities in our lives. I believe there is power in association. Who you hang around with is whom you will become like. I recently met a friend of mine who

I went to infant school with. Our families lived on the same street and as children we went to the same school and often played out on the streets together.

As we grew older, we went to separate secondary schools and became distant as friends. However, because we lived on the same street, we would still have a chat from time to time. As we matured into adults, we both moved from the location and went our separate ways, even though our families continued to live in the neighbourhood. As we were standing there chatting in the busy car park of Asda Supermarket, I learnt that she was getting married. She told me that after 21 years of living with her partner, they were finally "tying the knot." She went on to tell me that of her three children, the oldest was 21 and recently had a baby.

I was gob smacked. I said to her, "Do you mean you're a grandmother?!" and in my mind I was thinking *and I haven't even started yet*. I just couldn't believe it. We are both the same age, and the thought of me being a grandmother and having a son or daughter aged 21 was quite scary. There you have it: two people both in their forties, yet our paths took completely different turns. Her life could have easily been my life had I continued to keep company with those of a similar mindset.

Ladies, God is in control of each and every one of our lives. He has a specific purpose for you and me. Our destinies have already been written. If you are single now and it feels like you have been single forever and a day, try not to fret; it really isn't an accident. God knows what He is doing. He did not get your plans mixed up with somebody else's. Learn to trust Him. Why has my friend been a mother for 21 years and now is a grandmother as well, and I have yet to get on the ladder? Who can explain it, but I know that I do trust my future into His care. Would God deliberately hold back on us, perhaps out of spite? Absolutely, not! We should not view God through eyes that we perceive humans with. *Jeremiah 29:11* states, *"For I know the thoughts and plans that I have for you, says the Lord, thoughts and plans for welfare and peace <u>and not for evil</u>, to give you hope in your final outcome" (TAB)*. This is one of my favourite scriptures that I have lived by over the years, and one of the many I continually encourage myself with.

Also see what *Psalm 84:11* says: *"For the Lord God is a sun and shield: the Lord will give grace and glory: <u>no good thing will He withhold</u> from them that walk uprightly" (KJV)*.

Finally, as I close this book, I pray that its contents have given you some insightful tips as a mature single to encourage you in your Christian walk at this special season of your life. You are an awesome woman of God; therefore, walk tall with your head held high and with your dignity intact. Never let go of the fact that God has a special plan for your life. Remember that you have been in the making for 'such a time as this.' Live your life in a way that you will bring honour and glory to your Maker. Let your life be a picture of God and all His attributes. Let your life be like a letter for all to read about how God has kept and preserved you in such a fierce and competitive world. You are fearfully and wonderfully made in His image. Celebrate and enjoy your singleness, because it won't be long now before this season too will pass.

THE END

Bibliography

Chapter 2

[1 & 2] *Encyclopaedia of Questions and Answers. 2001 Octopus Publishing Group Ltd, Chancellor Press.*

Chapter 4

[1] *Dead Poet's Society (1989) - Directed by Peter Weir. Written by Tom Schulman and starring Actor, Robin Williams.*

Chapter 8

[1] *Reader's Digest Universal Dictionary, Berkeley Square, London, Harper Collins, 1987*

Chapter 9

[1] *Shakespeare, W. "Hamlet," Folger Shakespeare Library, Washington Square Press, New York, 1992.*

Chapter 12

[1] Raunikar, D. *"Choosing God's Best," Multnomah Publishers, Inc., 1998*

Chapter 14

[1] *Unknown*

Chapter 16

[1] *Chapman, Gary D. "The five love languages for singles," Northfield Publishing Chicago, 2004.*